Across the Land

One Man, One Mission, One Step at a Time

By Amy Fussell

To my dad, Jack Fussell,
Your determination, resilience, and heart inspired a journey that touched countless lives. This book is a testament to your courage and the legacy you left behind. Thank you for showing me that no mountain is too high, no challenge too great, and no dream too impossible.

And to my sons, Tyler and Ethan,
May you always walk with purpose, love with an open heart, and embrace the beauty of life's adventures.

This book is for the dreamers, the doers, and the believers, just like the three of you.

Amy

Introduction
A Journey Across the Land

Jack Fussell had a way of moving through life that defied expectations. It wasn't just that he crossed the United States on foot in 2013, though that feat alone turned heads and left people awestruck. It was why he did it, and the man he became in the process, that left an imprint far beyond the miles he traveled.

This wasn't a young man's impulsive adventure or an athlete's quest for glory. Jack, a retired insurance salesman, small business owner, and Navy Veteran, with a love for the outdoors, strapped on his walking shoes at the age of 62. His mission? To raise awareness for Alzheimer's

5

disease, the same illness that had taken his father from him years earlier. This journey wasn't born out of convenience or happenstance. It was a call to action, a way to honor his father's life while raising awareness about the disease that changed everything. Jack's trek across America wasn't just about walking; it was about listening, connecting, and proving that one person can make a difference, one step at a time. A way to give a voice to the countless families grappling with a disease that steals memories and erases connections.

The story you're about to read is more than a recounting of steps and miles. It's a tapestry woven from the threads of Jack's blog posts. His raw, unfiltered thoughts during his journey, and my own reflections as his daughter. This is the tale of an extraordinary man who turned heartbreak into purpose, one step at a time.

When Jack set out on that crisp January morning, the world felt impossibly large. By the time he reached the Pacific Ocean, it had grown smaller, kinder, and more connected, thanks to his unwavering determination and the strangers who joined him along the way.

So, lace up your shoes, dear reader. This isn't just Jack's journey, it's a walk for all of us.

Chapter 1
Roots and Reasons

Before Jack Fussell became the man walking *Across the Land*, he was a boy exploring the small town of Douglas, Georgia. Nestled in the heart of Coffee County, Douglas was a place where life 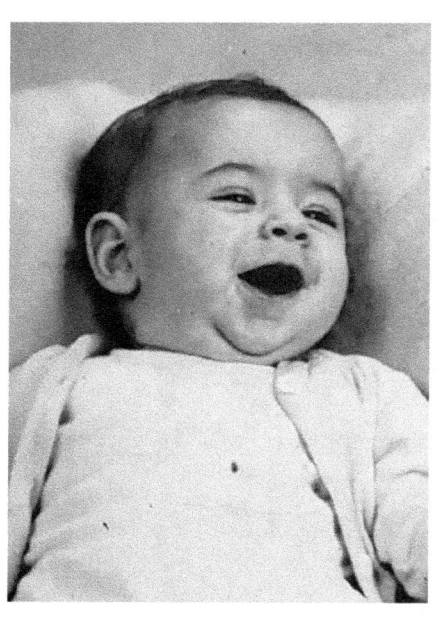 moved at a slower pace. Jack was born to Leonard and Maureen Fussell, a hardworking couple who dedicated themselves to doing the best they could and providing for their family.

As a child, Jack had an endless curiosity and energy that seemed to match the wide-open spaces of rural Georgia. But one ordinary day changed his life forever. The story, as I know it, is this: Dad was about three years old when tragedy struck. Papa (Leonard) was heading to the store, and Jack wanted to go along. Nana (Maureen) said no, but Jack ran outside anyway, hopping on his tricycle to follow the car. Papa didn't see him, and as he backed out of the driveway, he accidentally ran over him. I don't think Nana ever forgave herself, or Papa, for not noticing him that day. The injuries were severe, leaving Jack broken in both body and spirit. Doctors gave a grim prognosis: Jack would likely never walk again.

For a boy who had lived his life in constant motion, the idea of being confined was unthinkable. Yet, even as he lay in the hospital, his world seemingly shattered, a spark of determination burned within him. Jack wasn't one to accept limitations, not then, and not ever.

With the support of his parents and his own unyielding resolve, Jack began the long and grueling process of recovery. Every small movement was a triumph; every step, a victory. Slowly but surely, he defied the odds. By the time he was strong enough to walk again, Jack had learned one of life's most profound lessons: resilience isn't just about survival, it's about transformation.

The accident left its mark, not just on Jack's body but on his spirit as well. It taught him to face challenges head-on, to fight for what mattered, and to find strength in the face of adversity. What Jack didn't know at the time was that these lessons would fuel him in ways he couldn't yet imagine. The same resilience that helped him learn to walk again would one day drive him to walk across the entire country unassisted.

The lessons learned in his childhood would form the foundation of an unshakeable determination, shaping his ability to face the unimaginable journey he would undertake years later.

Chapter 2
A Life Reborn

"My dad passed away on June 30th of 2000. I was holding his hand. He died with Alzheimer's disease. Prior to that, prostate cancer had taken a huge toll on both his physical and his mental health. He was a veteran of World War II and witnessed a lot of injury and death. He was a great father. He taught my brother and I how to fish and how to play baseball. He loved making us laugh.

My relationship with Dad had been strained prior to his sickness (that strain was my fault). Immediately  following his passing, I realized the pettiness that kept me

11

away from time to time. Shortly after his death, I almost lost my life to a bleeding ulcer."

Jack's road to walking across America didn't begin with a simple desire to achieve something great. It started with a near-death experience that forced him to confront the most important question of his life: What was he willing to do with the time he had left?

In the year 2000, Jack was living a life that was far removed from the one he would later walk across the country to lead. He was 272 pounds, not caring for his health as he should have. But his wake-up call came in the form of a severe medical emergency: a bleeding ulcer that landed him in intensive care. The ulcer had cut through an artery, and Jack lost a dangerous amount of blood, his life hanging in the balance. Doctors gave him just two hours to live.

"I threw up about seven times in 45 minutes of just pure blood. So much blood," Jack recalled. But amid the chaos, as he lay in the hospital bed facing his mortality, Jack had an epiphany.

"I laid there a minute and I said, 'Lord, if you will save me, I will spend the rest of my life trying to help as many people as I can," he said. "I had no idea it would be about Alzheimer's, but I prayed that prayer."

By some miracle, Jack survived the night. But the doctors, who had been amazed at his recovery, gave him just one year to live. Determined to beat the odds again, Jack made a radical change. He adopted a strict pyramid diet of 1,800 calories per day, incorporating light weights and aerobics into his routine. His body, once sluggish and burdened, began to shed pounds. He dropped from 272 pounds to 155 pounds.

But more than the weight loss, Jack found something else during that recovery: a sense of purpose. The pain and loss of his father to Alzheimer's disease in 2000 had never fully healed, and Jack's brush with death renewed his desire to make a difference.

272 Pounds   155 Pounds

AcrossTheLand2013.com

He shed weight, adopted a healthier lifestyle, and gradually began to rebuild his body, but the true turning point came when he reached Amicalola Falls State Park in Georgia. Amicalola Falls, with its 729-foot cascade of water, became a symbol of Jack's journey, a place where he would push his body to its limits and redefine what was possible for him. At the time, Jack was still working to lose weight and gain strength, but running felt like an insurmountable challenge.

Instead, he set a series of goals designed to test his endurance and determination. The centerpiece of his training was the Amicalola Falls staircase, 604 steep steps, each one a test of his resolve. Jack committed himself to an ambitious plan: he would descend and ascend the stairs 25 times, then 30, then 35, 40, and eventually, 50 times. To Jack, one trip meant going down and up those 604 stairs, a total of 1,208 steps for every round. The effort was grueling, but Jack was determined.

In July 2011, he completed the ultimate challenge: 50 trips up and down the stairs in one day. That meant 17 hours and 18 minutes of climbing, step by step, each one a victory over fatigue, doubt, and pain. He made a card for every round and left them on

his car. After each round was complete, he would grab the

card for that number and

place it around his neck. He is

seen here with the card after

round 41.

During these intense

stair workouts, Jack learned to

push through physical and

mental barriers. Every climb

was a reminder that change was possible, even when it

seemed impossible. The stair training was not just about

getting stronger, it was about proving to himself that no

challenge was too great. It was during these long hours on the

stairs that Jack began to realize the power of persistence, of

setting goals and refusing to back down from them. His

weight was dropping, his strength was rising, and he felt

unstoppable. The state park sells shirts making a big deal

about climbing the stairs once, one way. He had just done it, round trip 50 times. After reaching this incredible milestone, Jack faced an unexpected emptiness. For the first time in years, he found himself without a clear goal in front of

him. The sense of purpose that had driven him to the stairs was gone. He prayed, reflecting on the journey that had brought him to this point, and talked to a few friends about what to do next. Then, one night, around 9:00 p.m., inspiration struck. Jack made a decision that would change the course of his life: he would walk across America.

Jack's journey across the United States wouldn't be easy, but it was the natural next step in his life. He had already proven to himself that he could overcome tremendous obstacles. Now, with a new purpose and a new goal, Jack was ready to take on the ultimate challenge.

Chapter 3
The Decision

Jack's decision to walk across America came to him like a calling. The moment he made the choice, everything seemed to fall into place. The ambition, the training, the goal, each one locked into his mind like a puzzle piece. He knew it was going to be a monumental challenge, but it felt right. There was no backing down now.

The moment that set everything in motion came unexpectedly. Jack was making calls to friends, telling them about his plans. One conversation took a turn that would change the direction of the entire journey. One of the people he spoke to asked, "What charity are you doing it for?" Without hesitation, Jack responded, "Alzheimer's."

It was in that instant, almost as if the words were spoken on their own, that Jack knew this was the cause he was meant to champion. It wasn't a decision he had consciously made before; his mind hadn't yet fixed on Alzheimer's. But when the words left his mouth, there was no doubt. He knew that his father's battle with Alzheimer's, and his own journey to help others, would drive him to go the distance. It was God's voice he had heard calling him, guiding him toward a cause that would become his life's mission.

At this point, Jack had spent years pushing himself beyond what seemed possible. But the idea of walking across the entire United States was daunting, even for someone as determined as Jack. He wasn't just setting out on a long walk; he was embarking on a mission. A mission to raise awareness for Alzheimer's disease, the disease that he believed needed more attention. He would walk for those affected by the disease, for his father, and for the countless others who struggled in silence.

Before setting out on his cross-country walk, Jack had a lot of planning to do. He needed to figure out logistics:

where to stop, what to carry, how to document the journey. And, of course, he wanted to raise money for the Alzheimer's Association. But Jack wasn't one to shy away from a challenge, no matter how overwhelming it seemed. He had already overcome so much, surely, he could walk across the nation.

The months that followed were filled with training, preparation, and anticipation. Jack had already proven his stamina by walking long distances, but now he had to build endurance for a much greater feat. He continued his walking and running routines, spending hours each day on the pavement, simulating the kind of physical demands he would face during his journey. Every mile added to his growing confidence, but he knew that the walk would test him in ways he could not yet understand, ways that he could not even imagine.

Jack also knew that this journey would require more than just physical endurance, it would require mental and emotional resilience. Walking across the country wasn't just about putting one foot in front of the other. It was about enduring the elements, the isolation, the doubt that could creep in when the road ahead seemed endless. It was about overcoming the internal battles as much as the physical ones.

Jack had faced his demons before, from the early trauma of being run over by his father to the near-death experience with his bleeding ulcer. Now, walking for Alzheimer's was his way of turning every past hardship into a stepping stone for the future.

As he prepared, Jack's resolve grew stronger. He was no longer just the man who had conquered the stairs at Amicalola Falls. He was a man on a mission, driven by the idea that even the toughest obstacles could be overcome with enough willpower.

In early 2013, Jack hit the road. With a simple stroller, backpack, phone, and his faith driving him forward, he set off from the East Coast to the West Coast. His walk wasn't just a physical challenge, it was an emotional and spiritual journey that would take him across thousands of miles, meeting people from all walks of life, and inspiring others to take control of their own lives, no matter what had happened to them in the past.

Along the way, Jack shared his story, speaking about his father's battle with Alzheimer's and raising awareness for the disease that had touched his life in such a profound way. He visited Alzheimer's support groups, met with people who had lost loved ones to the disease, and shared his journey with others who had similar stories.

As the days passed and the miles stacked up, Jack began to realize something even greater than the awareness he was raising, he was healing, too. Every step he took on that long road was a testament to the power of resilience, to the idea that life can change in an instant, but you always have the choice to keep going.

Chapter 4
The Preparation

As Jack set his sights on walking across America, the intensity of the task ahead began to settle in. The journey was not just a physical one; it required meticulous planning, careful preparation, and an unwavering belief in his goal. This wasn't a hike through a local park, it was an unprecedented trek across the country alone with the weight of his purpose and the enormity of the task, Jack knew he had to be prepared in every way possible.

He had set his mind on traveling unsupported, which meant no camper, no crew, and no team of helpers by his side. It would be him, the open road, and the mission at hand. The only consistent support he would have was from me, his daughter, from the other side of the phone and computer. We discussed everything in detail, the route, his supplies, the challenges he would face, and the ways we could stay connected. My role was to help with logistics, to offer encouragement, and to track his progress in real time, but I couldn't physically be there with him. This was his journey to walk alone, and as much as I wanted to be there to help him with the unknowns ahead, I knew this was the way he had to do it.

One of the first tasks was to gather the supplies Jack would need. As a seasoned walker, runner, and camper, Jack had an understanding of what gear he would require, but the difference now was that he would be carrying it all with him. Instead of relying on a support vehicle, Jack would load his jog stroller with everything he would need, water, food, clothes, tent, sleeping bag, tiny cookstove, maps, and, of course, his solar charger to keep his phone powered up for communication, updating his blog and emergency use. The stroller wasn't just for convenience; it became a crucial part of his journey, it was a jog stroller and he named it Wilson. It became a constant companion that helped him stay organized and prepared, even when the road stretched endlessly ahead of him.

And then there were the shirts, hats, and signs we designed together. The design was simple but crucial for safety. We chose safety yellow for the shirts and hats, with bold purple writing. We wanted every driver, every trucker, and every person passing by to see him clearly. I insisted on the bright yellow. It might seem like a small thing, but in my eyes, it was the only thing I could do to provide a teeny bit of protection to him. The roads he would walk on weren't always well lit, and not every driver would be paying close attention. The safety yellow would make him visible, and that gave me a little peace of mind.

It wasn't just the gear that needed attention, it was the logistics. Jack had no idea just how vital the little details would be once he started his trek. For instance, we set up a GPS tracker on his stroller.

This was an essential addition as it allowed me to check his location at any time, ensuring that if something went wrong, I'd be able to find him. It wasn't about tracking every step he took, but it gave me a layer of reassurance that, as much as he wanted to be independent, I wouldn't be left completely in the dark.

Another tool that helped keep us connected was the blog he created: the Jack Fussell Across the Land blog (https://jackfussellacrosstheland.wordpress.com).

He set it up to document his journey, to share his story, and to raise awareness for Alzheimer's. It was a place where people could follow along with his progress, read his updates, and offer their support. For Jack, the blog was a way to stay accountable to the cause, and for me, it was a way to stay connected to him. (As I write this now, I am even more grateful for the hours he spent posting and documenting his trip. It's in fact, the reason I am writing this. I want those memories to be there, to be able to be shared no matter what.)

As the days grew closer to his departure, one thing became overwhelmingly clear, Jack wasn't just preparing to walk across America, he was preparing to make his history. This journey wasn't about a man walking for the sake of walking. It was about the thousands of people who were affected by Alzheimer's disease, the countless families struggling with the loss of loved ones, and the desire to bring awareness to a cause that so desperately needed attention.

With everything in place, Jack took one final step into the unknown. No support vehicle, no crew, no

27

guarantees of what lay ahead, only the open road, his jog stroller, and the hope that every step would bring him closer to making a difference. And as much as we would all miss him, I knew that this was his journey to walk alone, a journey that would change not only his life but the lives of those who followed him.

As he walked across the country, Jack never lost sight of the promise he had made all those years ago, when he faced death on the hospital bed after his ulcer burst. With every mile he walked, Jack was keeping that promise, living out his commitment to a cause greater than himself.

Chapter 5
The Journey Begins

The first steps of any journey are often the hardest. But for Jack, those first steps meant something more, something larger than himself. As he walked out the door that morning, leaving behind the familiar comforts of home, he was stepping into the unknown, with nothing but his resolve and the open road ahead. His mission was clear: to raise awareness for Alzheimer's, to inspire others that it's never too late to make a change, and to prove that the strength of the human spirit could conquer even the longest of journeys.

I remember January 12, 2013 well, the day Jack left Skidaway Island State Park near Savannah, Georgia. It was early in the morning, the air crisp and cool, with the promise of an adventure just beginning. The bright safety yellow shirt gleamed under the blue sky, an extra measure of visibility.

The purple writing on the
shirt stood out against the
yellow, bold and
unmistakable.

We were all at the park

that morning, a group of

family and friends gathered to send him off on his adventure.

Most adorned in his shirts and holding signs. Some even

chose to run along with him for those first miles. This would

become a regular occurrence along his journey. People

jumping in and keeping him company for a few steps, others for a few miles.

And with that, Jack took his first steps out of the park, leaving behind the familiar for the long, uncertain road ahead. He left his stroller behind for the first  day, as he would be traveling a few miles into the heart of Savannah.

As Jack began jogging, Many stayed behind, holding our breath as he headed down the road. We could still see him in the distance, his yellow shirt a beacon of courage, and we all knew that this moment, this day, marked the beginning of something monumental.

From then on, I was always with him in spirit. The GPS tracker on his stroller became my window into his journey. I checked it regularly, monitoring his progress and ensuring that I always knew where he was. We spoke daily. Texting regularly as he did with key people that would enter his life over the course of this trip.

The early days were not easy. The miles stretched on endlessly, the exhaustion setting in quickly. These were long days of jogging, walking, pushing a stroller loaded with supplies, and dealing with the mental toll of the monotony. Jack was undeterred, his determination was steel, and no matter how difficult things got, he kept moving forward.

There was no turning back now.

Along the way, people would stop and ask about his journey. One of the first questions they asked was, "What are you walking for?" Jack would smile and explain that he was walking to raise awareness for Alzheimer's disease.

It was during those early encounters that the magnitude of what Jack was doing started to hit. He was really going to do it. The people who stopped to talk, whether they shared their own stories of Alzheimer's or just wished him well, reminded me that this wasn't just a personal mission for Jack. It was something much bigger. His walk was becoming a symbol of hope and resilience for people who were struggling with Alzheimer's and with mental health, as well as their families.

The trek would become grueling. The road would seem endless at times. But with every step Jack took, he grew stronger, both physically and mentally. There were days when it felt like the weight of the world was on his shoulders, but he never let that stop him. He kept pushing, even when the exhaustion set in. Because he knew that what he was doing mattered.

I watched Dad's progress on the giant U.S. map we had pinned to the wall. Each city Jack reached was marked with a pin, and the map began to fill up quickly. It was a tangible way for us to see his journey unfold, even from a distance. We would update it every day, it became a homeschool geography lesson. The map became a milestone tracker for the whole family, a visual representation of his strength and commitment.

The blog Jack had started was gaining momentum as well. Each day, as he walked, He updated the site with his progress, reflections from the road, and photos of the people he met. The blog became a lifeline for supporters, a way for people to follow his journey and offer their own words of encouragement. These also helped him, he enjoyed meeting new people and sharing stories, calling each one a new friend.

Jack's decision to go unsupported, without a crew or camper to help along the way, was one of the boldest aspects of the journey. He wanted to prove that, no matter what, he could rely on himself and the kindness of strangers. As much as he would let me, I tried to make sure everything was in place for him to keep going. I would call ahead of him to make contact with people in the areas he was heading to, so he could have a friendly face or two to keep eyes out for him, alerting media, trying to bring attention to the subject of his trip. The Alzheimer's Association was helpful with this as well, they would reach out to their local offices to meet with him and offer support as they could.

As he walked, Jack not only carried a message for Alzheimer's but also proved that it is never too late to make a change. Step by step, he was showing the world that the strength to transform one's life is always within reach, even if the path is long and the road ahead is uncertain.

Chapter 6
On the Road
January 2013

From the very beginning, strangers reached out in unexpected ways. In downtown Savannah, a man named Larry blessed him and told him God would be with him all the way to California. A group of four men in a pickup truck had seen him on the news and cheered him on. A police officer in Garden City checked in, making sure he was safe.

As he moved through Georgia, Jack found inspiration in everyday moments. A young man at a Baptist church in Statesboro invited him inside to rest and get water, his mother bringing lunch soon after. A gymnastics team gathered to pray for his journey. Along the way, people waved, honked, gave thumbs up, small gestures that meant everything. Some stopped to share their stories.

A man named Joey talked about his father, who had died three months prior from dementia. Joey told Jack how much he loved and missed him. Their connection was brief but profound, one of many that reaffirmed why Jack was making this journey.

Jack's journey was as much about remembering as it was about moving forward.

The support from strangers came in many forms. Meals were shared, a warm bed was offered, and contributions were made to the cause. A family at George L. Smith State Park provided fried chicken, chicken salad, and drinks after a long and exhausting day. A woman named Megan shared how her grandmother, lost to Alzheimer's, had once forgotten who she was.

One of the most moving encounters was with an elderly man who had lost his wife of 58 years to Alzheimer's. He had been driving down the road when he saw Jack, turned around, and stopped to talk. His grief was raw, his tears falling freely. Jack listened, offering what little comfort he could.

The physical demands of the journey were relentless. Pushing a 70-pound stroller loaded with supplies, he encountered long stretches of road with few people, aggressive dogs, and the ever-present threat of speeding cars on narrow shoulders. Some days were filled with conversation and companionship; others were lonely, with nothing but farmland and distant horizons.

By January 21, he had covered 150 miles, averaging around 15 to 20 miles per day. Some days stretched longer, with Jack pushing himself to 34 miles in one go. Other days, he allowed himself to rest, knowing that pacing himself was crucial for the months ahead.

Beyond the road, Jack took time to visit assisted living facilities and nursing homes. In Macon, Georgia, he met with Alzheimer's Association staff and volunteers. A surprise luncheon brought together people who shared their own heartbreaking experiences with the disease.

At Willow Pond Community, he had dinner with residents, many of whom had Alzheimer's. He noticed how they easily teared up when talking about their pasts, where they were from, how long they had been married, how many kids they had. Their prayers and well wishes for his journey resonated deeply.

He was struck by the caregivers he met, people like a woman in her thirties who had survived cancer and a stroke, yet still devoted her life to helping others. She had turned down a promotion and higher pay because she couldn't bear to leave the people she cared for.

As he walked, Jack reflected on how much he was learning, not just about Alzheimer's, but about resilience, generosity, and human connection. The road was harder than he expected, but the encouragement he received fueled him.

"I have become more determined than ever," he wrote. "I did not think that was possible."

He realized that this journey wasn't just about raising money or awareness, it was about people. Those he met along the way, those who had suffered loss, those who reached out to help him, even in small ways. He saw beauty in the kindness of a gas station worker, the generosity of a passing stranger, the silent support of a nod or a smile.

As January came to a close, Jack had covered 215 miles. His body ached, but his spirit remained unshaken. "I will never quit," he wrote. "We will find a cure. It is just a matter of time." And with that, he pressed forward, one step closer to California.

January 12, 2013

Entering Savannah from Skidaway State Park – Day 1

This is for the Alzheimer's Association. Met so many people that are trying to help.

At a church service letting out in downtown Savannah Larry saw me and came over and talked and told me God would bless me and that God would be with me all the way to California. God bless you Larry.

His posts were short and non-narrative in the early days, mainly photos and brief thoughts. He would post retrospectively and sometimes would repeat the same images. As much as the blog was a way to share, it was also and probably more so, a way to remember. Remembering why he was doing this.

January 14, 2013

Four Generations

US 80 is a very busy

highway. We were on the

shoulder most of the

time. Met some awesome people and had a lot of people

wave, blow horns and give me a thumbs up. Talked with

some wonderful people beside the road. Staying with my

wonderful cousin and her family tonight. The meal was so

good and the company even better. I'm doing well because of

all of the help that I am receiving.

January 15, 2013

Hardest Part

Leaving wonderful people.

Heading to California!!!!! 51 miles completed. I am Heading

to California. Running, Jogging, Walking and Talking. Raising

Awareness about Alzheimer's Disease. Raising Money for the Alzheimer's Association, so they can help people...

January 20, 2013

Harder to Do Than I Thought! This is harder than I knew. Visiting the nursing homes and assisted living facilities has made me know the disease is worse than I thought. More encouragement and support than I realized there would be. Because of the last two, I Am Stronger Than I Thought.

116 Miles done. Heading to California.

January 22, 2013

The Easiest State Resting today and thinking how all over Georgia I have kinfolk somewhere that could get to me in a few hours, if the need arises. When I get in the other states, it will not be that way. I will have to get mentally ready for that and become an excellent manager of both what I am doing and my emotions. Wow !!

January 23, 2013

171 miles done so far Heading to California. Raising money

for the Alzheimer's Association. Raising awareness about this

horrible disease.

January 24, 2013

Lots of Encouragement coming from the people with the

Alzheimer's Association

Short Day Today Short, 10 miles today. Getting ready to

meet my mom. She is in a lot of pain and under a doctor's

care. She Never Gives Up and Never Quits. She is the last of

a family of 13. She is 84.

January 25, 2013

This Is Just the Beginning I am only 62. I have, maybe,

another 48 years to set goals and do my best to Achieve

them. My plans are to live until I am around 110 years of age.

January 26, 2013

I thought I was meeting one lady for lunch. This awesome

group is what I found when I got to Golden Corral. These

fine people are Alzheimer's Association staff and Volunteers.

The Surprise Luncheon with the Macon Alzheimer's

Association. I thought my sister-in-law and I were meeting

one lady. It was a bunch of folks. All of the staff and

volunteers each stood up, one at a time, and told their stories

as related to Alzheimer's disease.

January 27, 2013

18 miles today. 199 miles so far It was an awesome day on US

Highway 80. Not much traffic. No-one stopped to talk. No

dog problems. Able to jog a good bit. Almost all folks moved

over to make passing me safer. A lot of waves and smiles. It was a beautiful jog/walk. My sister-in-law came out and picked me up. I will spend the night at her house tonight.

January 28, 2013

In Macon, Georgia. Ran, jogged and walked from Savannah to Macon, Georgia. I have been to several nursing homes, assisted living facilities and talked with people beside the road. Had a man run with me and a man be my support for about 3 miles. Been harassed by dogs. Stayed in my Bivy one night. Took days off, had a 34-mile day. Visited with family and friends. Been surprised at a meeting. It has been awesome.

January 29, 2013

16 miles today 215 total so far. Did not go by any nursing homes or assisted living facilities today. Wilson had a flat tire.

Chapter 7
Miles of Determination
February 2013

Jack Fussell pressed forward into February with a deepening sense of purpose and an ever-growing connection to those affected by Alzheimer's disease. With each mile, his journey became more than just a personal challenge, it was a mission to amplify the voices of those who had lost loved ones, to acknowledge the caregivers who fought battles of their own, and to ensure that the disease's devastating impact would not be ignored.

By the end of the month, he had crossed his first state, Georgia, covering 584 miles and raising nearly $14,000 for the Alzheimer's Association. He had visited four Alzheimer's Association offices, six state parks, and countless assisted living facilities and nursing homes. He had been met with open arms, heartfelt stories, and unwavering encouragement, but he had also faced the reality of the disease's reach, encountering pain that words couldn't fully capture.

February began with cold mornings, long miles, and new friendships. In Eatonton, he met Sonny and Janice Turner, who had lost family members to Alzheimer's. They hosted him for the night, and Jack was struck by their dedication to leading a support group for caregivers. These were the kinds of people who kept him going, people who understood the gravity of the disease and devoted their lives to helping others through it.

His sister-in-law Shirley, who had done more for their father than anyone else during his battle with Alzheimer's, continued to support him. Jack often thought about the reality of baby boomers aging and the looming Alzheimer's crisis that many experts feared. The more stories he heard along the way, the clearer it became that this wasn't a disease that could wait for a solution, it had to be addressed now.

Despite the emotional weight, Jack found moments of joy and strength. He and Wilson pushed through 56 miles in three days, despite temperatures as low as 24°F. He met a young couple who stopped for pictures, enjoyed coffee with a woman named Barbara who first thought Wilson was a baby stroller, and ran alongside new friends like Emily, who had driven an hour just to meet him.

In the early morning hours of February 7th, Jack woke up reflecting on a friend's question: "Don't you get tired?" His answer was simple: Yes, but I will make it to California.

Running an average of 17 miles per day, navigating roads, avoiding dogs, finding places to sleep, worrying about his family, and meeting new people only to say goodbye, was mentally and physically exhausting. But he thought about the caregivers he had met, the people who spent years watching their loved ones slip away. If they could keep going, so could he.

On February 12th, he hit 400 miles. The numbers were growing, but the weight of leaving Georgia behind started to settle in.

Jack spent time with our family before moving westward. Until that point, he had been running toward us, now, he was running away from us. That realization hit hard. He had trained himself to leave places, to keep moving forward, but goodbyes never got easier.

"This is how I feel. This is how I am. This is how it is supposed to be. It is supposed to be hard when you leave someone you love so much."

As he neared Dalton, Georgia, he passed the 500-mile mark. He met with the local Alzheimer's Association, visited nursing homes, and spoke with newspaper reporters who helped share his mission.

One woman in a nursing home in her late 80s shared a heartbreaking truth:

> "You will not see it when we have visitors, because we get excited when we have visitors, but sometimes some of us just bust out crying, because we get up each day, have hope for a couple of hours, and then it slowly fades away."

These words haunted Jack, reinforcing why he had to keep pushing forward.

On February 27th, Jack left Georgia behind.

"Georgia is done!!" he wrote.

He had fallen in love with so many people, and leaving them behind was harder than he had expected. But there was no time to dwell, Alabama was next.

The weather tested him immediately, cold winds, drizzle, mist, and even snowflakes fell as he entered his second state. The physical toll was real. He had developed a purple toe from hitting a step too hard, but he kept going. He pushed through an elevation gain of 1,900 feet into Cloudland Canyon and then onto Scottsboro, Alabama.

Along the way, people kept stopping to talk. They told him about their parents, siblings, and spouses who had been taken by Alzheimer's. He listened. He absorbed their pain. He carried it with him, mile after mile.

The numbers were growing:

- 606 miles covered
- $14,000 raised
- Countless hearts touched

And yet, Jack knew this was only the beginning.

February left Jack more committed than ever. At times, he questioned how much farther he could go, but then he remembered the faces of those he had met. The woman who said hope faded away. The man who had lost his wife of decades. The young woman who ran because her father, a former runner, could no longer do so.

This wasn't just about running across America anymore. This was a fight, a fight against a disease that had no survivors.

Jack had a long road ahead, but one thing was certain:

He would not quit.

Not today. Not ever.

February 1, 2013

Sad situations I guess it is normal. This trip at times can be very exciting and fun. Other times, it can be very sad. Hearing all the different stories from so many people. Seeing the pain in their faces, the tone of their voices and the tears. I want to become a better listener than I am. I can still remember who I am and where I am and who my children and grandchildren are.

February 2, 2013

Heading to Madison, Georgia

23 miles will be needed today by Wilson and I. Will be a very cold start, but we have to start early, so we do not have to run, jog or walk in the dark. It will be a beautiful day. I will try as hard as I can. I will do my best!!

23 miles today. 271 so far on the Journey So cold this am. 24 degrees. Beautiful scenery all the way. A young couple stopped and we took pictures. They were so nice. We made it.

Wilson and I are both tired.

February 3, 2013

Hard Labor Creek State Park

Need about 15 miles today to

get to the park. Wilson and I

will be on the road about 8:00

am.

15 miles today, 286 so far. Jogged and walked and talked with

Sam Moss today. Sam took over the controls of Wilson

today.

February 4, 2013

Barbara came out to the road to see if I had a baby in my

stroller. She then made us some coffee and we chatted a few

minutes in her carport. She showed me her dad's chickens.

19 miles today. 305 on Journey so far. Was a good day. Did

not pass any nursing homes or assisted living facilities. Felt

55

Strong today.

February 5, 2013

16 miles today. 321 miles for the Journey Great day, awesome people. The land was so beautiful. Lots of horses. Feeling Very Strong. Will see my daughter Sunday.

February 6, 2013

26 miles today. 347 for the Journey, Awesome day. No dogs. GNN radio interview. Fox 5 News interview.

Today was the best day I have had on this Journey, so far…..

February 7, 2013

4:00am Woke up thinking of a question a friend called and asked me a few hours ago. Don't you get tired? I do. I will be 63 in October. On the days I am running, jogging and walking, I am averaging 17 miles a day. On those days I am on and off the road and the shoulder, watching out for dogs and cars and trucks, making sure I am going the right way, wondering where I will sleep, wondering about my family and burning calories. I am constantly meeting new people, falling in love with them and then leaving them, probably to never see them again. On the days I do not run, jog and walk, I visit nursing homes, assisted living facilities and Alzheimer's Association offices. I bet caretakers get tired, but they keep on going!! Yes, I get tired and yes, I Will Make It to California. Raising awareness about a horrible disease and raising money for the Alzheimer's Association

February 8, 2013

Friday, February 8th Starting near Cumming, Georgia. Heading towards Canton, Georgia. Gonna be an Awesome day. Wilson is raring to go.

17 miles today. 364 for the Journey. Awesome day. 3 different people ran with me.

February 9, 2013

21 miles today, 385 for the Journey from Skidaway Island State Park to here 385 Awesome miles.

February 10, 2013

Goals are an important part of everyday life…No matter how big or small, GOALS come into play every day. It is not just about reaching those goals. It is about rising above them. We are the only ones that truly prevent ourselves from reaching our goals. It is within each and every one of us to accomplish whatever our heart desires.

7 miles today. 392 on the Journey. An Awesome day. Breakfast with a friend. Ran with Family and Friends right up to my daughter's front door. Debbie here too. Wish my son could have been.

February 11, 2013

Not Running Today!! I am at my daughter's house. I ran to her house yesterday. Going to do some planning today. Will run a little today in the neighborhood, hopefully with my Grandsons.

February 12, 2013

400 Miles We just hit 400 miles on the Journey so far.

18 miles today. 410 miles of the Journey complete. An Awesome day. Strong. Lots of encouragement.

February 13, 2013

19 miles today. 429 for the Journey. Very Encouraging day for me. Started off with Some members of the Reinhardt University Cross County Team going with me a couple of miles. Had 5 or 6 people stop and talk to me. Did not like leaving the Haney's house. I felt so at home there and

enjoyed all of the little guys.

These Awesome people were waiting for me when I started running this morning. This is in Waleska, Georgia. These are students at Reinhardt University. Awesome people.

There will be a day when I can no longer run. Today is not that day.

February 14, 2013

429 miles of the Journey is complete Starting somewhere in the mountains and ending somewhere in the mountains today.

16 miles today. 448 for the Journey. Started very early. Very cold. Shoulder pretty wet. Invited in for Coffee. Lots of waves. Very encouraging for me.

February 15, 2013

My Dear Friend "Wilson" He is helping me go Across the Land. We are Fighting the Alzheimer's disease.

Broken toe?? Wednesday night, I hit my middle toe on my left foot on a step. It is kind of purple now. I did 16 miles with it yesterday. It hurt a little. I will do the next 100 miles or so with a purple toe.

My Dear Precious Amy. Up to this point, I have been Running to her. From this point on, I will be running away from her. That will make it very hard for me. This is how I feel. This is how I am. This is how it is supposed to be. It is supposed to be hard when you leave someone you love so much.

I somehow missed this post, as I sit here with misty eyes, I realize he did this a lot. These trips aren't for the faint of heart. Not knowing where you will sleep, who will cross your path, not an easy task. He did it his way. I'm proud of him. Trips like this don't just affect the runner, they also affect their family, their kids, grandkids, parents, friends. But they also impact strangers. Family members have to support, a calling is a calling.

February 16, 2013

My son Jack, I have not seen my son that lives in Copenhagen, Denmark in a long time. I just spoke with him on the phone for 1/2 hour. He used the time to encourage me. He told me about a time I said something that caused him to search within himself and that helped him do what he is doing today. He is an Awesome young man and I wish I could see him today.

February 17, 2013

I am sitting here posting this note with my smartphone. Sad, because I am leaving people I love for a few months. That is okay, that is who I am. No saying or quote can change that. I know me well, of course, and I know tonight I will pack my friend Wilson and tomorrow morning we will head West together. Wilson will carry the load for me and I will push for Wilson. I will think often of those I love deeply. I will be scared some and will remember to turn my fears over to God after a while each day. One day maybe I will not forget to do that all of the time. It is an Awesome Life we all have. I love mine, every day of it. "I can do all things through Christ that strengthens me."

February 18, 2013

$10,000.00 Andrea from the Alzheimer's Association called and said we hit the $10,000.00 mark with donations. Thanks to everyone from the depths of my heart.

February 19, 2013

18 Tough miles tomorrow there is a lot of up hills on tomorrow's run. Going up 52 to almost the other side.

February 20, 2013

Alzheimer's Ninety percent of what we know about Alzheimer's has been discovered in the last 15 years. Some of the most remarkable progress has shed light on how Alzheimer's affects the brain, thanks to dedicated researchers like Dr. Morgan. His team is now targeting the tangles of proteins called tau that build up inside brain cells more rapidly in people with Alzheimer's than in the general population.

Rough day climbing Fort Mountain. Steep roads, wind, cold. Ice and snow beside the Road.

February 21, 2013

Heading to Dalton, Georgia. I will pass the 500-mile mark today.

20 miles today. Not much climbing to do. Dalton has an Alzheimer's Association office. I hope to visit.

February 22, 2013

Dalton, Georgia Will meet some more with the Alzheimer's Association. Every time I do this I learn even more about dedication and compassion. Will visit some assisted living or nursing homes. This teaches me more than I could say here.

February 23, 2013

Ringold, Georgia. Short 17 miles today to Ringold today. It will be good.

Trip Getting Tougher, I will too.

21 miles today. 529 miles for the Journey Biggest day for folks stopping to talk and horn blowing and waves. Very

encouraging.

February 24, 2013

529 miles of experience. Realized this morning that I have 43 days of experience running with Wilson. I have a lifetime of help with my life. Even though I may not have thought it, I have always needed people to help me. I have always needed God.

Time for Camping. At first, I thought I would camp out a lot. That was okay. The way it looks now, I will have done the almost 600 miles of Georgia spending the night only 1 time in my tent. Looking at Alabama, and the trouble it will cause others to find places for me to stay, my mindset is going back to looking at a good bit of camping. I know this. Wilson and I will go out into the Pacific Ocean together.

16 miles today. 545 for the Journey Awesome day. Lots of waves and horns. People stopping today to thank me.

February 26, 2013

22 miles today. 567 for the Journey Hard day. Drizzle and misting all day. Windy and an elevation gain of around 1900 ft. It was a good day.

February 27, 2013

Alzheimer's Day at the Capital. Wish I could be there. This is an awful disease that is getting huge and causing devastating things to happen to families.

A new state.....Alabama 2013

17 miles today. 584 for the Journey. Awesome day. Everyone everywhere so encouraging.

Georgia is done!! Started at Skidaway Island State Park on January 12th, 2013. Went 584 miles. Visited 4 Alzheimer's Association offices. Visited 6 Georgia State Parks. Visited many nursing homes, assisted living facilities and 1 senior day care facility. Met many wonderful people. All have been wonderful. Fell in love with so many people. We have raised almost $14,000.00 in donations for the Alzheimer's Association. Surely this team effort has raised awareness. Been an Awesome Journey.

February 28, 2013

22 miles today. 606 miles for the Journey.

Chapter 8
Winds of Change
March 2013

Jack and Wilson entered March with new milestones, new states, and an unwavering resolve to bring attention to the fight against Alzheimer's disease. Each day on the road, he encountered people whose lives had been shaped by the disease, patients, caregivers, family members, all carrying their own pain, loss, and determination.

By the end of the month, he had run, jogged, and walked through Alabama, Mississippi, and into Tennessee and Arkansas, covering nearly 940 miles. His journey had become a moving conversation about Alzheimer's, connecting him with communities, news stations, support groups, and everyday people who simply needed someone to listen.

The weather was relentless in March. Cold winds, torrential rain, hail, lightning, and even snow flurries tested Jack's endurance. Running on unfamiliar roads with no shelter in sight, he often found himself forced to pause, though only when absolutely necessary.

One of the hardest moments came on March 5th, when a powerful storm rolled through. The day started with wind, then rain, then lightning, and finally hail. It was dangerous, but Jack pushed forward, determined to reach his goal of 20 miles. Brandy, from the Alzheimer's Association, called to check on him. Concerned for his safety, she and Courtney made the call to pick him up. Jack, a man who rarely stopped moving, accepted their help, but only because it meant he could fight another day. He wrote: "20% of the journey done. Fighting a fight against Alzheimer's disease."

The storm left him physically exhausted, but it was the unpaid caregivers he had met along the way that kept him going.

"I will run all day in the rain. My shoes and feet will be soaking wet. But this is nothing compared to what unpaid caregivers experience every day."

Despite the physical toll, Jack never entertained the idea of quitting. Instead, he used the discomfort as motivation. His aches and fatigue were nothing compared to the endless heartbreak of those caring for loved ones with Alzheimer's.

Jack's mission was clear, to fight Alzheimer's, to raise money, and to let people know they weren't alone. Everywhere he went, he met people who shared their stories. Some stopped him beside the road. Others welcomed him into their homes, offered food, or simply waved and honked as he passed.

In Scottsboro, Alabama, he sat with a man who spoke with pride about his past, until the conversation turned to his late wife, lost to Alzheimer's. The sadness washed over him instantly. His voice changed, his shoulders dropped, and he walked away without another word.

In Huntsville, Jack attended his first Alzheimer's support group meeting. What he saw there shook him, people exhausted, broken, desperate for help, many of them unpaid caregivers who had given everything to care for someone they loved.

Jack felt helpless.

"Please tell me what more I can do," he wrote. "I will make it to California, no doubt. I will continue to try to help fight Alzheimer's long after this journey is over."

The miles kept adding up.

- March 12 – 700 miles crossed

- March 15 – Entered Mississippi

- March 21 – Entered Tennessee

- March 26 – Entered Arkansas

- March 27 – 900 miles crossed

Each new state was a celebration, marked by a photo of Wilson in front of the state line. But with each new state came more painful goodbyes.

One of the hardest came on March 13, when he had to leave John and Valerie McAbee, a couple who had taken him in and cared for him like family. Their kindness had become a lifeline, and moving forward without them left a hollow feeling.

"The hardest part isn't the running. It's falling in love with people and having to leave them."

As the journey gained more attention, people began making pledge donations per mile. Some gave $5 per mile, some $3, others $1, but every step Jack took now had an extra layer of meaning.

One man called Jack late one night and promised $5 per mile for a full day's run. Jack pushed hard, logging 23 miles that day, earning $115 for the Alzheimer's Association.

Then, on March 13, nine more people pledged to do the same.

- $935 raised in one day
- 17 miles completed that day

These moments fueled Jack, they reminded him that he wasn't running alone.

"This is not and never will be a race. It is a fight to stop Alzheimer's disease."

With every step, Jack found himself reflecting more deeply on his father. On March 19th, after passing the 800-mile mark, he wrote a letter to him:

> "Dad, I hope you are proud of me. Mom told me the other day that she was. I am trying really hard to help in the fight against Alzheimer's disease. I love you, Dad. Tell my brother Denny hello for me."

He thought about the small things, playing baseball together, fishing, watching his dad chat with his friends while getting the oil changed. All of it felt so close and yet so far.

He also thought about his mother, who was in constant pain but refused to let him quit. He called her one night, ready to stop everything and come see her. She told him: "Keep running." So, he did.

The end of March saw Jack and Wilson continuing toward Little Rock, Arkansas.

- 937 miles completed
- 13 TV appearances
- 7 magazine features
- 9 radio interviews
- 400+ roadside conversations about Alzheimer's
- Over $15,000 raised

But the journey wasn't about numbers. It was about the unpaid caregivers he met in support groups. It was about the man who cried over his wife's failing memory. It was about the countless people who had lost a parent, a sibling, a spouse. It was about the runners who joined him, even if just for a few miles. Jack wasn't just running to California. He was running for them.

"If we help one person get help, and raise $1.00 for the Alzheimer's Association to help that person, we are successful."

And with that, he kept going.

One step closer.

Each step west.

March 1, 2013

Just got a tweet from someone saying we passed the $15,000.00 amount. That is pretty cool. Thanks to you guys that have helped.

12 miles today, 618 miles for the Journey Cold, windy, some flurries. Lots of waves, no dogs. Awesome Day.

March 2, 2013

I recently sat with a man and listened to him speak of things he had done that he seemed very proud of. He smiled and looked all around and held his head high. Then, in a flash, he looked straight into my eyes and everything about him seemed to change. He looked sad and let his shoulders droop a little. He told me how long his spouse had been gone and that she died from Alzheimer's disease. He got up, shook my hand, wished me luck on my journey and walked away.

March 3, 2013

22 miles today. 640 miles for the Journey. The Day was beautiful. It was cold. The area I ran through was also Beautiful

March 4, 2013

My first Support Group I attended a support group meeting in Huntsville, Alabama today. It was my first. So many people affected by this terrible disease. I felt so sorry for the attendees. Non-paid caretakers, that are trying to take care of someone they love.

March 5, 2013

14 miles today. 654 for the Journey. Wanted 20, but weather got rough. 20% of the Journey done. Fighting a fight against Alzheimer's disease.

March 6, 2013

20 miles today. 674 for the Journey Early Start, lots of wind. I am tired. Beautiful country here. Awesome people. Wilson performed very well.

Hard Day. Did it for the Alzheimer's Association So cold with winds gusting 15 – 25 miles per hour. The rain yesterday, the lightning and the hail wore me down.

March 7, 2013

Day 64

9.14 weeks. 674 miles.

74 miles per week.

6:30am. Decatur, Alabama

Not Feeling Well

March 10, 2013

Work up not sure if phone clock had changed by itself or not.

It did. Today I see Brandi one more time. Will be hard saying

goodbye to another Awesome Alzheimer's Association

person.

19 miles today. 693 for the Journey

Beautiful day. Lots of wind. Lots of open country.

March 11, 2013

Not Running due to weather. Rain all day not a real problem.

Possible thunderstorm's is a problem. Stayin put with John

and Valerie McAbee.

March 12, 2013

She wants a divorce

The gentleman cried as he told me, he has been married for

46 years and his wife says she hates him and wants a divorce

several times a week and then a few hours later, she does not even remember anything about it. He looks so tired and so hurt and helpless. He does not know what to do. He said they used to go shopping and she would tell him to sit on a bench and rest and she would come get him "atter while"

Two Awesome Months

693 miles on foot. Visited 5 Alzheimer's Association offices. Met Amazing and Wonderful people in each one. Visited countless Assisted Living and Nursing Homes. Stopped beside the road and talked with countless people with connections to the Alzheimer's disease. Alzheimer's disease and the Run has been highlighted on 7 TV stations, 5 radio programs and almost every newspaper in every town Wilson has been through. You have donated over $15,000.00 to the Alzheimer's Association. I have had 26 people run with me. We Are Doing Well. I have had so much help from Amazing and Awesome People. I love every one of you. Thank you for Fighting Alzheimer's Disease.

March 12, 2013

23 miles for the day. 716 for the Journey Beautiful Day, no clouds. Cool. Some wind. Awesome road to be on. Hwy 72. Wonderful folks. Lots of waves, horn honking and folks stopping.

March 13, 2013

17 miles today. 733 for the Journey.

It was hard leaving Valerie and John this morning. Such wonderful people. Beautiful day. Wind, but no clouds. Lots of encouragement from drivers. Lots of encouragement from friends and family. Awesome Day.

March 14, 2013

15 miles today. 748 for the Journey. Beautiful day. Clear sky. Lots of horn blowing and waves. Lots of folks stopped to talk. Felt Great.

March 15, 2013

Mississippi, here we come. Wilson and I are pretty excited

about the run today. Going into

our third state. Will get a good

picture of that sign.

You carry the load. I will push

buddy. We will go to California.

We will go out in the ocean. Then, we will both go home..

A new state…. Mississippi 2013

March 16, 2013

We will be heading to Corinth, Mississippi today. Going to be

Beautiful. I will have company. My host for the last few days

will be walking with me.

17 miles today. 781 for the Journey

Beautiful Day. Awesome weather.

March 17, 2013

Not Running today. Resting my body and mind. Gonna be Beautiful. Heading towards 800 miles.

March 18, 2013

Severe Thunderstorms

Lightning just started. Wilson says he is not going out in this stuff..

Hardest Part. Falling in love with people and having to leave them.

March 20, 2013

Starting near Walnut, Mississippi and about 22 miles today. Weather gonna be Awesome. Wilson and I will do our best!

21 miles for the day. 824, for the Journey. Beautiful day. Blue Sky. Windy. Little cold in the morning. People were all

Awesome. Met all 3 people from the Alzheimer's Association office. Visited the Carriage Court Assisted Living Center in Memphis. The run is about 22 miles outside of Collierville, Mississippi. Wilson and I will run into Tennessee tomorrow.

March 21, 2013

Will Run into Tennessee today. Going to be Beautiful. Will be an Awesome Day.

March 23, 2013

Feeling Strong!! Doing my best every day. Feeling good. Feeling strong. My Resolve to help has never been as Strong. I will Never Quit trying to do my Best!

March 24, 2013

A new state…..

Tennessee 2013

18 miles today.

862 for the Journey. Cold, wet, windy. Ran with Awesome runners. Drivers fantastic. Law Enforcement folks were so Awesome. We had a cool guy supporting us today and taking pictures.

March 26, 2013

A new state….. Arkansas 2013

14 miles today. 876 for the Journey. Cool. Not much wind.

Sunny. Awesome people. Several stopped. In Arkansas now.

March 27, 2013

Long Day today. Backtracking a little this morning, with the

help of a family heading to Atlanta. Taking me back to cover

4 miles I missed yesterday. I need about 26 miles today. JUST

DO IT !!

Dogs Just had about a 10-minute serious encounter with

dogs. All okay!

24 miles today. 900 for the Journey

Blue sky. Not much wind. Mild temperatures. Great drivers. 6

people stopped to say hello. 1 man pulled and handed me 2

bottles of water.

March 28, 2013

19 miles for the day. 919 for the Journey. Clear skies. Mild

temperature. No wind. 6 folks stopped and spoke with me

today. Newspaper interview today.

March 29, 2013

Not Running today. Rain, with possible thunderstorms. I
don't run in lightning. I have though, but not now, not today!
Days like this are tough. Right now, it is partly sunny.
Forecast shows off and on thunderstorms today. 26 miles for
the next Run. Open farmland all the way. No place to take
shelter when lightning starts. Decision to stay put, but I don't
like it. Just read some articles about running in lightning and
they reinforced what is in my gut.

March 31, 2013

Running towards Little Rock, Arkansas

Bad Weather

Torrential Rain. Lighting far off.

18 miles today. 937 for the Journey. Cloudy, sprinkling rain.

Nice folks waving, blowing horns and moving over when

they could. Weather turned bad fast. A man took me in and I

was fine.

Chapter 9
Turning Point
April 2013

April was a month of milestones, both physical and emotional. Dad crossed state lines, reaching Arkansas and then Oklahoma, but more importantly, he crossed into the hearts of hundreds of people. Every step he took was another opportunity to share his mission, to meet someone who needed to talk, and to remind himself why he had set out on this journey in the first place.

There were days of triumph, days of exhaustion, and days when life pulled him in a different direction entirely. But through it all, he kept moving, because that's what he did.

Early in the month, Dad hit a major milestone: 1,000 miles. He had been on the road for over three months, pushing his jogging stroller, Wilson, across the country. He celebrated the achievement quietly, with gratitude, acknowledging that there were still thousands more to go.

It was about the moments. The people. He met a road crew who gave him doughnuts and chicken. A small grocery store where the cashier refused to let him pay. Fifteen people stopped one day to talk, each with their own connection to Alzheimer's. Some had lost loved ones. Some were still fighting. Some just needed to be heard.

One of the most powerful encounters happened in Memphis. A homeless man saw Dad jogging and called him over. His hands were shaking, his voice unsteady, but he listened as Dad told him about Alzheimer's and why he was running. Without hesitation, the man reached into his pocket, pulled out the last $20 he had, and handed it to Jack. *"Donate it,"* he said. It was in moments like this that Dad knew, what he was doing mattered.

Running across the country wasn't just about putting one foot in front of the other. It was about stopping, too.

In Lonoke, Arkansas, Dad spent time at a nursing home, sharing breakfast with residents. He met a woman in her 90s, proud of her children, still telling their stories. Another woman, nearly 100, exercised every day. He saw how the staff cared for their residents with love and dedication. *"This is an eye-opening event for me,"* he wrote.

He attended Chamber of Commerce meetings, spoke on the radio, and met researchers like Dr. Steve Barger in Little Rock, who was dedicating his life to finding a cure for Alzheimer's. These stops gave him a sense of balance. They reminded him that the fight was bigger than his journey, it was a collective mission.

But rest, for him, was never truly resting. Even on his "off" days, he was working to spread awareness.

Then came the call.

His stepdad, Jack, was in the hospital. His mother, already in pain from her hip, was struggling.

Without hesitation, he rerouted. He rented a car and drove 1,500 miles back to Valdosta, Georgia. It wasn't a question of *if* he would go, it was a matter of *how fast* he could get there.

Dad struggled with this, the tension between home and the road. He had a family. People he loved. And yet, he felt in his soul that he had to keep going. Nana understood. As they sat together, she looked at him and said, *"Glad you're here, but you gotta go back pretty soon and finish the job."*

That was all he needed to hear.

While in Georgia, he kept moving in his own way, spreading awareness at gas stations, fast food places, and even giving a talk at a local school. He knew that if he stopped for too long, the mission might lose momentum. And he wasn't willing to let that happen.

By the end of the month, he was back in Arkansas, stepping into Oklahoma with over 1,200 miles behind him.

The road stretched ahead, long and uncertain, but he never doubted that it was the right one.

April taught him more than he expected. He saw kindness in its purest form. He learned that no matter how tired or broken he felt, his spirit was always stronger. And he saw, in the faces of those he met, that Alzheimer's wasn't just a disease, it was a daily battle for millions of families.

He closed the month with a simple but powerful reminder: *"Keep going. That is what we do. No matter how tired we get, how upset we get, how disappointed we get. We keep going."* And so, he did.

April 1, 2013

30 miles today. 967 for the Journey. Beautiful weather. 70

degrees, no clouds, just a breeze. Awesome people.

Strong Spirit

My spirit is indeed stronger than my body. 30 miles took its

toll, but I will leave tomorrow morning for 21 more miles. I

am pretty proud of the 30 miles today.

April 2, 2013

23 miles today. 990 miles for the Journey Cold, cloudy, windy

and finally wet. Awesome day to be Fighting Alzheimer's

disease. 10 people stopped and talked.

April 4, 2013

My daughter Amy, recently said "dad, if you help one person,

it is worth it"

April 5, 2013

Little Rock, here we come.

We made it guys.

16 miles today. 1006

for the Journey Blue

skies, no wind, mild temperatures. 12 people stopped to talk.

Went over 1000 miles today.

April 6, 2013

Dr. Steve Barger Running in the Capital City Classic 10k. This

was a Huge Race, almost 800 Runners. Bill Torrey talked

about what we are doing to Fight Alzheimer's just before he

started the race. Got to meet the Legendary Bill Torrey.

April 7, 2013

Just talked with my mom. She could not hardly talk. She is at the emergency room with my step dad. She had to go. I called our family friend that lives in the same town with mom and Jack. She is heading to the hospital now and will call me when she gets there and finds out something. Jack is a U.S. Navy veteran of World War Two. Jack is 84 years old. She told me a few minutes ago that he has been stuttering the past couple of days and cannot walk straight. This morning, mom got a neighbor to come over and they talked mom's husband into going to the emergency room. They have admitted him. I am considering taking a bus home for a couple of days to see my mom…

This was often something I watched dad struggle with. He knew that life continued to move forward, even if he wasn't "home". It was hard to be away. But he knew the journey was worth it. He had to live for himself, he had to do what he felt in his heart was right, even if it meant not being home.

Wilson and I will be back. Someone from the Alzheimer's Association will be picking me up shortly to take me to get a rental car. I will drive to Valdosta, Georgia to see my mom for a couple of days. I will then return to Little Rock, Arkansas and Wilson and I will go to California.

April 8, 2013

Birmingham, Alabama

Continuing my mission on the detour I've had lots of time to think while I am driving to Valdosta and I am continuing my mission on this short detour. I am still wearing my "uniform" Across the Land shirt. I am still talking to people everywhere

I stop – McDonald's, gas stations, etc. No reason to let these opportunities to reach people – and tell them about the Alzheimer's Association and how terrible this disease is – pass by.

Mom and her son. I made it to Valdosta, Georgia.

April 9, 2013

In Valdosta, Georgia. Still do not know much about what happened to mom's husband Jack. He is still in the hospital. Mom is in constant pain. Hard on her.

April 10, 2013

I will be in Little Rock Arkansas tomorrow around noon. I will start running Saturday morning. Wilson And I are heading to California.

Part of the Across the Land 2013 crew. (*Dad was very proud of his grandkids.*)

April 12, 2013

Back in Arkansas today. We Will arrive in Arkansas this morning. Saturday morning, Wilson and I will be back on the Road again, pressing on to Monterey, California. Fighting

Alzheimer's disease.

April 13, 2013

Arkansas Running this Morning through Little Rock. Great weather. Good to be back. Feeling Very Strong. This Is Important. It Matters. People Are Hurting. We Gotta Help.

16 miles today. 1024 for the Journey. Beautiful weather. Awesome company. Great people all the way.

April 14, 2013

A Good Question:_A young man and his wife stopped and said thanks for caring. He asked if it is worth it. I told Yes!! This is hard, but it is worth it.

16 miles Today. 1040 for the Journey People were all so nice.

April 15, 2013

University of Arkansas of Medical Sciences

I attended two events today at the University. It was truly a day to remember. I first attended a PhD students dissertation defense, which was very interesting. I also attended an event that included a screening of a segment of the Charlie Rose piece on Alzheimer's. This was part of a 5-week series. I learned a lot about what the medical community knows about Alzheimer's. I learned that staying healthy and keeping blood pressure and cholesterol under control can definitely be helpful in reducing the likelihood of Alzheimer's. Dr. Jeanne Wei and Dr. Steve Barger both told the crowd about my journey and how important awareness is. That is one of the reasons I am going Across the Land. The other is to raise funds so the Alzheimer's Association can continue to provide support, information and fund research to end Alzheimer's. I was asked to say a few words and I told the crowd how important the research work they are doing is to helping the people that stop me on the road each day. And the people all over the country that are dealing with this horrible disease.

With your support, we'll make a difference in the fight.

April 16, 2013

16 miles. 1056 for the Journey. Beautiful Day Wonderful

People all over. Talked to 17 people about Alzheimer's.

1 Newspaper interview. Ran Hard, one foot in front of the

other.

April 17, 2013

5 people so far today have talked with me beside the road. I

enjoy them.

18 miles today. 1074 for the Journey. Ended up in Morrilton,

Arkansas

April 18, 2013

I am in Morrilton, Arkansas. Not Running today. Bad
weather predicted. Will be spending most of the day at a
facility for seniors.

April 19, 2013

27 miles today. 1101 for the Journey

April 20, 2013

28 miles today. 1129 for the Journey Weather just right.

No dog problems.

Beautiful area.

Lots of bicycles.

April 21, 2013

Sunday, April 21, 2013 #ENDALZ Going to Sharpen the

Saw today. (rest) Thinking about my dad. He died with

Alzheimer's disease.

April 22, 2013

Normal Is Overrated!! #ENDALZ We can Slow and then

Stop Alzheimer's. This Journey is not a normal thing to be

doing, but it is helping, because people care !!

26 miles Today. 1155 for the Journey in Ozark, Arkansas

tonight. Beautiful weather.

Talked with 13 people.

April 23, 2013

17 miles Today. 1172 miles for the Journey. Cloudy weather

Great driver's beautiful land

April 24, 2013

Not Running Today. #ENDALZ Spending the day with the

Northwest Arkansas Alzheimer's Association Folks. Full day,

trying to spread the word about the help available from the

Alzheimer's Association.

April 26, 2013

Friday, April 26th, 2013. Not Running Today. Will be talking

and sharing with residents and staff at Legacy Heights

Retirement Center in Van Buren, Arkansas. Will be spending

time the people at the Fort Smith, Arkansas office of the

Alzheimer's Association.

April 27, 2013

My Thoughts Tonight. Sunday Morning, I will finish my Run

into Fort Smith, Arkansas. Monday, I will Run into

Oklahoma. I keep thinking back to the Determination God put in me. Ran over by a car at age 3. Not supposed to walk again. Pneumonia 4 times. Bleeding ulcer at age 51. Told I may not live another year. Lost 100 lbs. in a year. That was 12 years ago. Went 1172 miles so far, pushing a 70 lb. jogging stroller Across America. Fighting Alzheimer's disease. I will stop when I hit the Pacific Ocean. After that, I will do something else.

April 28, 2013

Heading west, one step at a time!!

21 miles today. 1193 for the Journey

Beautiful weather beautiful scenery

Awesome people 26 cars stopped today Foot doing Well !!

April 29, 2013

Heading to Sallisaw, Oklahoma. Need 23 miles. The weather forecast is for a high of 86 degrees. Will be on Hwy 64.

A new state.

Oklahoma 2013

1200 miles done

A new born - A man

stopped me to tell me his precious grandchild was born 3

hours after his dad died from Alzheimer's disease!!

24 miles today.

1217 miles for the Journey

86 degrees for the high

Blue sky

April 30, 2013

23 miles today. 1240 miles for the Journey

85 degrees for the high

Blue sky

109 days into the Journey.

Chapter 10
The Heart of the Journey
May 2013

May was a month of deep endurance, powerful connection, and a growing sense that this journey was becoming something greater than miles and memories. Dad's legs stayed strong, but it was his heart that carried him. He passed through Oklahoma, connecting with families, caregivers, researchers, and supporters who all had one thing in common: a story touched by Alzheimer's. With each step westward, the message grew louder, there is help, there is hope, and we must not give up.

Dad began the month feeling strong. From Greenleaf State Park to Muskogee, Tulsa, and on through Oklahoma City, he ran in all kinds of weather, hot sun, heavy winds, and bone-chilling cold. Despite it all, he pressed forward, logging hundreds of miles. He ran on Route 66, spoke to anyone who would listen, and often handed out Alzheimer's bracelets and cards with the 1-800-272-3900 helpline number.

He stayed in nursing homes and assisted living centers where he ate breakfast with residents, heard their stories, and witnessed firsthand the impact of the disease. One morning, he watched a man repeatedly reach toward a vending machine, not understanding why he couldn't grab the drinks. It broke his heart, but it also fueled his fire.

In Tulsa, the Alzheimer's Association threw their support behind him with interviews, health fairs, and community outreach. They helped him repair Wilson and made sure he had what he needed. People gave him places to stay, meals, hugs, encouragement, and sometimes, even just a few minutes of conversation that made all the difference.

Throughout the month, Dad emphasized the importance of unpaid caregivers. He reflected on their long hours, the emotional toll, and how their efforts often go unseen. He made plans for "The Longest Day" in June, pledging to walk or run for 16 straight hours in honor of those who give so much, every single day.

He also shared stories of people who had lost loved ones to Alzheimer's, including a man who had been married for 66 years and had just lost his wife. Another woman recalled her husband being "gone for seven years, but dead for two."

Dad talked about the need for more research funding. He pointed out the massive discrepancy between what was spent on Alzheimer's compared to other diseases, and he dreamed of the day when there would be a National Alzheimer's Institute to help coordinate the fight.

Midway through the month, tragedy struck. A devastating tornado hit Moore, Oklahoma, just a few miles from where Dad was staying. He didn't run that day. Instead, he stayed close, listened to people's stories, shared tears, and did what he could to comfort them. He texted donations to the Red Cross and Salvation Army and encouraged others to take action too.

The experience humbled him. It reminded him, once again, of the strength of the human spirit and the importance of being present, not just on the road, but in people's lives.

By the end of May, he had passed the 1,500-mile mark. He was more than halfway to California. A route change was planned, one that would take him through Amarillo, Albuquerque, and across the Mojave Desert. He consulted with other ultrarunners for guidance and began preparing for the harsh, hot terrain ahead.

His reflections became more frequent. He pondered how this journey had changed him. He noticed more beside the road, places to hide in case of hail, places to rest, places where someone might need him. He noticed the kindness of strangers. The determination of caregivers. The resilience of those fighting Alzheimer's. And still, he kept going.

"I can for sure, help one more person," he wrote. That belief carried him every day.

He saw himself not as a hero, but as a messenger. A man walking for a cause he believed in. A man who had lost his own father to Alzheimer's and couldn't bear to watch others suffer in silence. He wanted them to know they weren't alone. That help existed. That someone cared.

"If it's worthwhile, do it," he wrote. "Never stop trying. Be a good example." And he was. With every mile, every conversation, every quiet act of kindness, he was the example.

1,610 miles down. 1,392 to go. The road was long, but the message was clear: Keep going. It matters.

May 1, 2013

Heading West #ENDALZ

12 miles for the day, 1252 for the Journey, 85 degrees for the high, blue skies, Little windy, beautiful scenery, Awesome people, 4 cars pulled over.

May 3, 2013

Lost my battery backups

Wilson fell on his side because I was on a steep shoulder and the wind caught him. I thought I picked up everything. When I got down the road aways, I went to get my backup battery kit. It was not there. I caught a ride very quickly and went back about 5 miles to get it. I Found it. Getting a ride back did not work. So, I am hoofing it back now. Gave up on getting a ride. This is just part of it. No problem. Lost time and miles, but that is okay. One step at a time Heading West!! Fighting Alzheimer's disease !!

Awesome Week. 124 miles in the last 6 days. #ENDALZ

FIGHTING Alzheimer's disease with every step!!

May 5, 2013

Heading West, Sunday, May 5th, 2013 #ENDALZ Not

Running today. I am in Tulsa. The Run is actually in Coweta,

Oklahoma, just east of Tulsa.  I will be resting my body today. I will be visiting with as many people as possible and

talking about Alzheimer's disease with them.

My Journey Across the Land. #ENDALZ Running, Jogging and Walking Across the United States of America. Pushing a jogging stroller named Wilson. Raising money to help the Alzheimer's Association, help people. Letting people that need help concerning Alzheimer's, know the Alzheimer's

Association can help you. Please call 1-800-272-3900 for help, anytime. I will listen to your story concerning Alzheimer's disease.

May 6, 2013

Dr. Steve Barger. #ENDALZ Thank you for trying to find a cure for Alzheimer's disease.

Thanks for the $2000.00 donation to the Alzheimer's
Association Senior Star #ENDALZ

May 7, 2013

Across the Land's Mission. #ENDALZ To let people know
the Alzheimer's Association exists. To raise money so the
Alzheimer's Association can help people, once they know
about them. To get people to tell the United States Congress
we need more money for research.

May 8, 2013

17 miles for the day, 1320 for the Journey, 84 degrees for the
high, Clear skies most of the day, beautiful scenery
Awesome people, talked to about 29 folks today about
Alzheimer's disease, gave out 16 cards, Gave out 21 bracelets.

May 9, 2013

91-year-old Gentleman. #ENDALZ He came over to speak

to me. He lost his wife to Alzheimer's disease a few short weeks ago. They were married for 66 years. He said it is a "Terrible" disease. He said this is hard to go through.

Keep Going!! #ENDALZ A gentle lady told me this evening that Alzheimer's took her husband. She said he has been dead 2 years, but gone for 7 years. She said it was tough for her because her buddy did not know her anymore. She exclaimed to me, "why can't they find a damn cure?"

May 10, 2013

One Step at a Time, Heading West. #ENDALZ Heading out around 8:30 am. Will go about 16 – 18 miles today. Going through Sapulpa, Oklahoma. Route 66.

119

Route 66 again today. Short day. About 14 miles. Weather mostly good. Chance of thunder storm.

May 12, 2013

We are heading West. One Step at a Time

19 Miles for the Day. 1379 for the Journey. Had breakfast with the residents at Rainbow Assisted Living in Bristow, Oklahoma. Took off around 9:00 am on Route 66. Found segments of the Original Route 66 and Wilson and I got on it some. It was a good feeling being on Route 66, I guess because I have heard of it all of my life. Gave out 6 cards and 11 bracelets promoting the Alzheimer's Association. It was a

good day. I feel good and I feel thankful for still having my

mother. I am in Stroud, Oklahoma for the night.

May 13, 2013

What is the Most Important. #ENDALZ Recently, a TV

reporter asked me, off camera, if I only had one thing to say

to the public, what would it be? I told him to tell the public

about the 1-800-272-3900 phone number that you can call 24

hours a day, 7 days a week, if you need help concerning

Alzheimer's disease. This number will be answered by the

Alzheimer's Association.

May 14, 2013

Very caring people!! I was pushing up a very long and steep hill today. The temperature was almost 90 degrees. Wilson felt heavy. In a short stretch, I had 3 people stop their cars and ask me if I needed help getting up the hill. I thanked each one and kept pushing. These people made me feel good.

May 15, 2013

The Most Important Number. #ENDALZ For help concerning Alzheimer's disease Call. 1-800-272-3900

The halfway point. Amarillo, Texas is pretty close to being the halfway point on this Journey of 3500 miles.

Senator Crain with the Oklahoma State Senate He introduced the Journey to the Oklahoma State Senate. It was such an honor for me.

May 16, 2013

Mark Bravo It was pleasure meeting Mark and talking and even running with him a few feet at the capital yesterday. He is very inspiring. He gave me a copy of his book "MOMENTUM". Mark is a runner!!

My Advice!! If it is Worthwhile, do it. Never stop trying!

May 17, 2013

Alzheimer's disease is Huge!! I have seen firsthand the amount of construction going on all across the country to accommodate the unbelievable growth of Alzheimer's disease. This disease, besides hurting families so bad, is gonna cost Medicare and Medicaid more than we can afford. Good gracious, it seems like we have to do something.

May 18, 2013

Saturday, May 18, 2013 Recap #ENDALZ Wilson and I

cranked out 18 miles today. 1433 miles done so far on the Journey. 95 degrees today. Not much wind. Lots of Awesome Sunshine. Drank a lot of water today. Thanks to Randle Lee with the Alzheimer's Association for breakfast and providing shuttle service. Staying at Touchmark again tonight in Edmonds, Oklahoma.

May 19, 2013

Sunday, May 19th 2013 #ENDALZ Still heading west to California. Loving every minute of Living. Trying to help people. Trying to tell people about the Alzheimer's Association. Trying to get donations for the Alzheimer's Association. Staying Strong!!

A First for us. Wilson and I went through a canal to avoid storm damage. This was kinda hard on us both!!

May 20, 2013

Many lives were changed today and there was a large loss of life. I will stay here and talk and maybe cry with people that have lived here most of their lives. These are my feelings and what I will be doing tomorrow. I will be in Mustang spending the day with staff and residents that I want to be near.

May 22, 2013

We are trying to help fight Alzheimer's disease. 80,000. Thank you for the 80,000 hits on the web site. You guys are all so Awesome.

My Age!! Some days I feel my age. Not today. Today, I feel older !!

May 23, 2013 Feeling my normal age!! Woke up raring to go. Feeling 30 years old again.

Thank You Very Much. I know that I ask so much, from so many on this Journey. I know it probably puts pressure on you. I also know without your help; I would have to quit. I also know that will not happen. We are a team trying to affect something that needs to be affected. We are letting people that need help, concerning Alzheimer's disease, know that help is available. We are raising money for the Alzheimer's Association so they can provide that help. Thank You All!!

468,000 new Alzheimer's patients every year #ENDALZ if the costs, in total, are predicted to be $50,000.00 per person, per year. My calculator will not handle that.....

May 24, 2013

Lost a friend. #ENDALZ I lost a friend a few short years ago. He took his own life. He was developing dementia. He was concerned for his family. SB315, recently signed into law in Oklahoma, could, possibly have helped.

Thanks to Paul Staso. #ENDALZ Thanks for sharing your thoughts with us all, concerning your many Long-Distance Runs. Reading your entries has been extremely helpful to me.

May 25, 2013

Heading West. #ENDALZ One step at a time. I need 25

miles today.

1500 miles

All Done for the Day. #ENDALZ 28 miles today, 1,521.

This bridge was almost 3,500 feet long. Not much traffic

though.

May 26, 2013

This Team Has Accomplished Much!! #ENDALZ It is 2:27

am. Lots of good thoughts in my head. We have raised close

to $25,000.00 for the Alzheimer's Association. That Will

Help!! We have told hundreds of people the Alzheimer's

Association exists and gave them a way to get in touch with

them. That Will Help!! We have been on many local news shows and in countless newspapers talking about Alzheimer's disease. That shows caregivers that we are trying. It shows thousands of people, we care.

May 29, 2013

Route Change #ENDALZ We are making a route change

that will take effect upon leaving Amarillo, Texas.

May 30th, 2013

#ENDALZ Heading west about 20 miles. Good weather predicted.

May 31, 2013

Got to control myself better. When my phone died today, I instantly realized my GPS, and phone numbers were in the phone. To someone watching me, they would probably have not seen anything. Inside, I was close to a panic. This will make me stronger!!

Chapter 11
Through the Fire
June 2013

June was a month of extremes, of heat, emotion, and sheer determination. It tested Dad in ways the previous months hadn't. The roads grew hotter, the distances longer, and the terrain more isolated. But his mission never wavered. With Wilson at his side and his purpose in his heart, he pushed west through Texas and into the deserts of New Mexico, driven by one thought: unpaid caregivers face harder days than this.

He entered Texas on June 2, with 1,633 miles behind him. It felt like a milestone worth celebrating, and he did, in the simplest way: by keeping his feet moving. Through small towns like Shamrock, McLean, Alanreed, and Groom, he pressed on under a relentless sun, temperatures often climbing into the 90s. At every stop, he encountered people who reminded him why he was out there. At the Midpoint Café in Adrian, when he needed a place to stay and something to eat, strangers stepped in. "Great people everywhere," he wrote. "Ever since the beginning."

Texas also brought bigger cities and deeper connections. In Amarillo, he met with staff from the local Alzheimer's Association chapter. He stayed at The Cottages at Quail Creek, spent time with caregivers, and reflected on the toll the disease takes, not just on those diagnosed, but on those who love and care for them. "I can leave at any time," he wrote. "Caregivers can't."

His body was holding up, but the environment was taking its toll. He began to take rest days more intentionally. "Sharpening the saw," he called it. When the temperatures soared and the elevation climbed, he listened to his body and leaned on the people around him.

June 21st, The Longest Day, was a pivotal point. For 14 hours, he walked, ran, and pushed Wilson through blistering heat, trying to honor the unrelenting dedication of caregivers. Around mile 27 of a planned 31-mile day, everything changed. Disoriented and confused, he found himself in the middle of the road, narrowly missed by semi-trucks. Dad called me, and our recollection of this event is similar yet different. I vividly remember him calling and I could hear the horns honking in the background. He told me they were giving him thumbs up and waving, he felt encouraged by them.

In reality, he was walking in the road and they were honking at him, he was in a bad position and I recall asking him to see if there was any shade around him. He stayed on the phone with me and told me there was one small bush. I advised him to go sit by it and I'd call him back in a moment. I immediately called the New Mexico police and informed them of the situation. They knew about him and his trip and didn't hesitate to go pick him up. They called me back after dropping him off at the hotel and asked me if I wanted them to insist on taking him to the hospital. I felt secure in dad's decision and respected it so I told them no and expressed my gratitude. That day was the most afraid for him I had been since he began this trip.

He didn't finish the 16 hours. But he survived, and that mattered more. "I'm good with this," he wrote. "I did my best."

He rested for several days afterward, reflecting on the experience and debating whether or not to continue. "I will pray, talk with trusted advisors, family and friends… I will make this decision. I will be the one that lives with it."

By the end of the month, he was back on the road, crossing into New Mexico and logging his 2,000th mile. The landscape changed. The land stretched flat and barren for miles, with few trees, fewer people, and hardly any shade. He loved it. "Sometimes I find myself searching for these times," he wrote, remembering the peace he felt in the silence of the land.

Still, the challenges remained real. The high altitude, lack of water, and blistering sun made each mile harder than the last. I became the lead coordinator for logistics, hotel stays, supplies, safety checks. "I don't want to die," he wrote bluntly. "This is very serious out here."

But amid the danger, there was beauty. A young boy wished him luck. A man stopped just to hand him a cold bottle of water. A woman named Savanah showed up at 6:29 AM, just as promised, to shuttle him to the starting point for the day. A stranger from Griffin, Georgia reminded him just how small the world could be.

By June 30, he stood in Albuquerque, New Mexico. 2,005 miles completed. Less than 1,000 to go. He had changed, not just physically, but emotionally, spiritually. He had faced exhaustion, confusion, even danger, and still chose to keep going.

His purpose was still clear. "The journey was two-fold from the beginning," he wrote. "To help with the fight against Alzheimer's disease, and to show it is never too late to change."

And as always, he ended with the simple words that had carried him through every mile:

"One step at a time, heading west."

June 1, 2013

#ENDALZ Today is the 140th day of the Journey. We have taken off days to try and help the Alzheimer's Association, with awareness. We took off days due to sickness. We took off days to drive over 1500 miles to visit with my mom. We have taken off days to simply rest my body and my mind. Wilson and I have traveled together 1,610 miles on this Journey. We have averaged close to 12 miles per day, for all days. This includes days we did not run. We have averaged close to 22 miles per day, on days we have run. I probably have jogged and ran about 1/2 of the time. I have no pain or health issues. We have had a lot of help, from a lot of people. It is too hard to name them all.

June 2, 2013

I will give out, before I give up .. on anything worthwhile. I want to be a good example!!

7:00 am. We are leaving for Shamrock, Texas!!

A new state.....Texas 2013

No matter what occurs. #ENDALZ It doesn't matter what happens. Somehow, I keep on going, day after day, week after week. 141 days, 1,633 miles Just like unpaid caregivers.

June 3

Thumbs up?? #ENDALZ Out here I see a lot of people giving me thumbs up and have folks give me fist bumps. Wonder how many caregivers get that? I will think of this the next time I see one.

Heading to Monterey, California

#ENDALZ 21 miles covered today. 1654 for the Journey.

1348 miles left. From Shamrock, Texas to McLean, Texas.

High was 90. Windy. Clear skies. Left Shamrock at 7:00 am.

Arrived in McLean around 1:45 pm

Paul Staso – The Best…. #ENDALZ Our Journey is soon to

take us on some long days and very serious heat. Very

dangerous heat. Paul Staso is the best Extreme Long-

Distance runner I have read about. Paul is helping me with

advice and planning for this Awesome part. I am 62 years old

and will do the very best I can, every day…..

States we have been through. #ENDALZ, Georgia, Alabama, Mississippi, Tennessee (corner), Arkansas, Oklahoma, Texas. (now in Texas)

I know I am blessed to still Run #ENDALZ

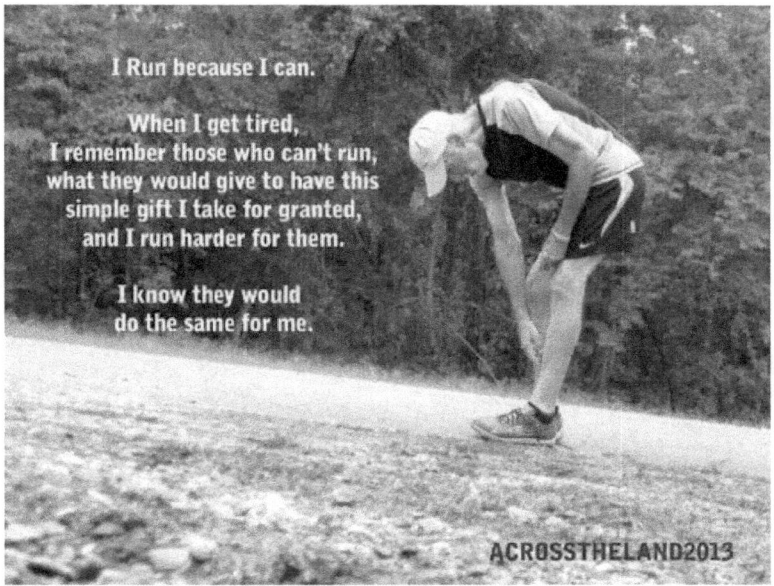

June 4, 2013

A lot of peace out here. #ENDALZ

Wade, the computer guy. #ENDALZ I appreciate his help with this Journey. He drove to Northeast Alabama to meet me for the first time, all the way from Daytona Beach, Fla.

He put a tremendous amount of work into the website. He

found me many places to rest my body at night. He set up

events to build awareness for the Fight with Alzheimer's

disease. He did more. I hope he feels realizes how much he

has done. Thank You Wade!

June 5, 2013

23 miles for the day. 1,686 for the Journey. 1316 left Sunny

today. High near 80 degrees. Not much wind. Saw a dead

rattlesnake. Drivers were great again.

June 6, 2013

16 miles today, 1 702 for the Journey. Around 80 degrees for the high No clouds No wind. Beautiful farm land. Great drivers.

June 7, 2013

Heading into Amarillo, Texas #ENDALZ Going to be a Great Day. Get to meet the lady with the Alzheimer's Association in Amarillo today !!

22 miles today, 1,724 for the Journey. 1278 miles left. Left Conway, Texas this morning at 5:30 am. Made it to Amarillo,

Texas around 12:35 pm High of 80 degrees. No clouds. High winds. Staying at The Cottages at Quail Creek.

Lorry is the Executive Director at The Cottages at Quail Creek.

June 8, 2013

Alzheimer's disease. #ENDALZ I am near it a lot these days. I can't imagine what it must be like to be with people that have it, every day. I think it is even very hard on paid caregivers. I feel like I can see the stress in their facial expressions.

Sharpening the Saw. I am very tired, physically and mentally. I will sleep, get up, get dressed and head west!!

June 9, 2013

Been A Great Week!! #ENDALZ We logged in 102 miles this week. Heading West, one step at a time!! Our story was in a couple of newspapers and on one TV station. Giving out

the number 1-800-272-3900

June 11, 2013

We are in Wildorado, Texas

17 miles for the day. 1752 for the Journey. 1250 left. High on

me was 93 degrees. Strong head wind.

No clouds. Awesome drivers From Amarillo to Wildorado,

Texas.

Thursday, June 13th done for the day. #ENDALZ 24 miles today. 1,790 for the Journey. 1212 miles left. High of 101 degrees today. 10 mile per hour head wind. Sunny all day. First time on a dirt service road. Had to dodge cactus and Spanish bayonets. Major heat. I feel Strong !!

Resting in the Community Center

Today, when it was 101 degrees, I came to a ridge and stopped and saw there was no shade anywhere to be seen. I felt some fresh asphalt sticking to my shoes. I reached inside of me, into my heart and I smiled. I turned the iPod on and started running. It felt grand. I feel strong!!

June 14, 2013

A new state…..New Mexico 2013

June 15, 2013

Saturday, June 15th, 2013 Not running today. Resting my body and my mind. Yesterday was a Hard Day for me!! I will be on the road tomorrow !!

June 16, 2013

Father's Day; Happy Father's Day!!

25 miles today

Heading to Tucumcari, New Mexico

No matter what occurs #ENDALZ Wilson and I keep on

going. One Step at a Time, heading west.

We just keep going and going!!

90,251 hits on the website #ENDALZ

My day today Started at 6:00am. I noticed that I could start as early as 5:30am. I got lucky, about the time the sun would start hitting me pretty hard, some clouds appeared and helped for about 1.5 hours. Also stopped every hour to rest in shade for 10 minutes. Drank water every hour. 25 miles was no problem. It was a good day.

June 17, 2013

Shopping list: Axe handle for critters. Snake bite kit. More lights for Wilson. Reflective tape for Wilson.

The dog bite from Friday is healing fine. I made sure the pup's shots were up to date, irrigated it and it is doing well.

The dog was huge and vicious. (Chihuahua)

June 18, 2013

The clouds finally burned off and it turned into a beautiful day. The landscape is also beautiful. I have not experienced land so flat and barren. It has its own special attraction. It makes me wish I could show it to my family and friends and let them feel like I feel. There were a lot of waves, thumbs ups and honks today. I enjoy this part. I spoke with a journey biker today. He is pedaling across America, in honor of his grandmother, that died from cancer. I seem strong, both physically and mentally. I feel like I did a good job today. I feel proud.

June 20, 2013

The Longest Day is tomorrow. #ENDALZ Wilson and I will attempt to go for 16 hours tomorrow. I will think of as many of the caregivers as I can remember while we are on the move. Caregiving is not something that I have ever done. My brother Denny and his wife Shirley took care of my dad. On this Journey, I have felt, just moments, of what it must be like. My cap is off to you caregivers. It looks like it is so hard, both physically and emotionally.

I want to still be running at age 100. 38 more years.

Wilson has close to 2,400 miles logged. Training miles and Journey miles.

Wilson, and his buddy, Jack.

June 21, 2013

Starting the Longest Day now. #ENDALZ 16 hours.

Friday morning, June 21st. I started pushing Wilson at 5:00 am. I knew we had 31 miles to go. I knew the high temperature would get near 100 degrees. I had already seen on Google Maps, that I would be climbing most of the day and there would not be much shade available.

I felt like from my past history, that I could make it, or I would not have attempted it.

I drank about 24 ounces of water per hour. Any shade I came upon, I got in it for a few minutes. I walked most of the distance and jogged some.

Around mile marker 27 of the 31, I needed, I started feeling weak and got under an overpass for about 15 minutes, to get out of the sun. I drank some and poured water on my body, in an attempt to keep my core temperature down.

I started back and immediately hit a gentle, but long uphill. In a few minutes I heard semi horns blowing and looked up to see a semi going to my left to avoid me and one going to my right, to do the same. I was totally confused as to why I was in the middle of road.

I headed for the shoulder, and a couple of cars swerved to avoid me. I called Cyndie, my daughter (Amy) and Paul Staso to alert them. They all responded, trying so hard to help someone very far away. I left Wilson on the shoulder and went to the shade of a very small tree and sat and cried. I am not sure why the emotions, but they were there.

All 3 folks continued to call me trying to help. I was having a hard time understanding them and they later told me I sounded very disoriented. They got in touch with the New Mexico State Police. In a few minutes they showed up. He made sure I was okay, as best he could. We loaded up Wilson and he drove me to a hotel. He wanted to take me to a hospital but I turned that down.

I rested a little, took a cool shower, ate some and drank. My urine was pretty clear, my pulse was 60. My skin felt okay, not too hot. I noticed a white chalky substance on my legs and was pretty sure it was probably salt leaving my body.

My nephew Kevin phoned from Georgia

He tried to figure out what might have happened. He thinks I lost too much salt. Salt helps the brain fire and without it causes confusion. I had no chest pain, no shortness of breath, just the confusion and exhaustion.

I am resting for 3-4 days in a hotel. The weather is going to get much hotter and I will need to do even more climbing with Wilson. The land will get even more barren than now. Not many resources out here.

I have a major decision to make. I was the only one there. I have been the only one on the trip.. I have put every ounce of "push" available to me, in this trip.

I will pray, talk with trusted advisors, family and friends over the next two days.

I will make this decision. I will be the one that lives with it. That is my responsibility. I will do the very best I can.

June 22, 2013

I did not complete the 16 hours. I completed 14 hours. I am good with this.

June 23, 2013

Sunday morning!! It is great to be out here in New Mexico. A short explanation of what I am doing #ENDALZ Tuesday morning, June 25th, I will load Wilson and my gear into a car. We will head west, approximately 28 miles. I will get out of the car, snap Wilson upright, load him up with my gear and head west. We are heading to Monterey, California. We are trying to raise awareness concerning Alzheimer's disease, trying to let people know the Alzheimer's Association exists and trying to raise money for the Alzheimer's Association.

June 24, 2013

Stay Alive, Be Healthy, Finish. #ENDALZ The mantra for the rest of the Journey. Serious conditions out here. Heat, lack of shade, lack of water. We will get this thing done!! All of us. Thanks for the help in fighting Alzheimer's disease.

June 25, 2013

Plan: One Step at a Time, Heading West !!

This is the type of shade available out here.

It was a good day today. We thought about today's plan very thoroughly. Taking into account my shuttles schedule, what happened Friday, the forecast for today and the lack of resources out here, we planned a short run. It was just right. I felt good when I started this morning and I still do. It has been fun interacting with folks here this afternoon. I will go about 17 miles tomorrow.

In my bivy, good night. Gotta get some sleep. I am getting old. New Mexico sunset. Very beautiful.

June 26, 2013

Done for the day!! I am in Moriarty, New Mexico. Wow, I am beat. The Run is at Clines Corners

The reason this is kicking me so hard Very high temperature is one reason. Another reason is the altitude. I have been, running, jogging and walking in 98 – 105-degree air temps with my higher pavement temperatures. I have been climbing also. I am almost 7,000 feet high. This combination is tough on me. It wears me out.

June 27, 2013

Marcia Bobo and Leo Beller These two supporters of the Journey and close friends, have offered their services to us again. Marcia has been a huge supporter since before I took the first step heading to Monterey. Leo (her husband) came on board later. They have contacted my daughter Amy and offered to come out and be a support crew through the dangerous area, I am getting ready to enter. Marcia, Leo and Amy are working out the details now. I appreciate the sacrifice they will be making.

I will not be running today!! Going to rest my body and mind today. I need to adjust to the temperatures and the elevation changes. I Will Adjust and Will Finish This!!

No Support After I posted that Marcia Bobo and Leo Beller were coming out to provide support for me, I felt very uncomfortable. I begin to examine my feelings and thoughts. I realized I was not doing what is in my heart with this. I was giving into being afraid of the unknown. Maybe being afraid that I would not control myself enough on a daily or even hourly basis to finish the Journey safely. I do not want any harm done to my health. I want to be strong mentally and physically. I want to control my emotions. I just had a long talk with Marcia Bobo and she understands. She also said if I need them at some point, they will come.

June 28, 2013

Good Morning. Friday Heading West, feeling good. Fighting Alzheimer's disease

21 miles today. Will hit 2000 tomorrow !!

36 miles until I enter Albuquerque, New Mexico. Over 1/2 way through this state.

June 29, 2013

I sure hope this helps someone. #ENDALZ I really hope all this effort by us all helps in some way. Not because I want to feel helpful, but because I hope people that are hurting, get some help, so they can at least feel like someone cares about them.

Today, I will pass the 2,000-mile mark.

Heading out to Albuquerque, New Mexico.

2,000 miles done…..cool…

2005 miles done 997 miles left on the trip. It was a fun day. A lot of people stopped to talk. Chatted with a cool sheriff's deputy. Just a fun day with beautiful views everywhere. Hitting the 2000-mile mark was so much fun.

June 30th 2013

Looks like the weather is gonna be nice. Kinda hot, but still nice. Very beautiful area I am in now. My first time in Albuquerque. I will meet another Alzheimer's Association staff member this morning. Hope you have a good day.

Done with Running for today!!

The next part of the Journey we will focus on is from

Albuquerque to Gallop, New Mexico. This will be fun!!

Chapter 12
Still Heading West
July 2013

July brought emotional highs, physical strain, and hard decisions, each one shaping the final leg of Dad's journey across America. From the heart of Albuquerque to the mountainous roads of Arizona, he kept moving forward, step by step, never forgetting why he began: to fight for families battling Alzheimer's.

The month began in Albuquerque, where Dad connected with the local Alzheimer's Association chapter and received incredible support from their team. They treated him like family, offering rides, rest, and encouragement. He met Governor Susana Martinez and Mayor Richard Berry, thanking them for their support of Alzheimer's initiatives like the Silver Alert system. He spoke at St. Pius High School and ran with the cross-country team, humbled by their energy and strength.

But something shifted inside him. He missed home deeply, his family, friends, and especially his grandkids. He spent July 4th remembering the fireworks and Waffle House breakfasts back in Georgia. The isolation and the miles weighed heavily on his spirit.

For a moment, he considered ending the journey. And yet… he couldn't. Not yet. "I have done everything I could to try and pretend I do not miss my family and friends. No matter what I do, I still miss them so much. But I am still out here."

Leaving Albuquerque, he entered some of the hottest, most rugged parts of the trip. The temperatures soared above 100°F. Water became harder to come by. His Achilles tendon throbbed. His mind was tired. Still, he pushed through mile after mile, talking to everyone who would listen about

Alzheimer's, often giving out the 1-800-272-3900 helpline number and sharing stories from the road.

In one unforgettable moment, he walked past a man who looked quiet and sad. When Dad asked how he was doing, the man simply said, "Right now, I am struggling." They shook hands and shared a human moment of truth. Two strangers, both fighting unseen battles.

Even while Dad struggled physically, he stayed committed to lifting others. "This is hard," he wrote. "But caregivers don't get to choose when to quit."

Midway through July, Dad traveled to Monument Valley, Utah, standing where Forrest Gump famously stopped running. The symbolism was not lost on him. He felt something there, maybe peace, maybe purpose. It gave him just enough clarity to decide: he would not quit. Not yet.

Back in New Mexico, he rested, regrouped, and took a hard look at what it would take to finish. He'd already gone more than 2,000 miles. There were 826 left. With new gear and a renewed spirit, he made the decision: "I will rest, plan, and finish this job."

By the end of the month, Dad was in Arizona, climbing higher into the mountains near Flagstaff. Despite the altitude and heat, he remained determined. He met with staff at Alzheimer's care facilities, shared meals with new friends, and received hugs and prayers from strangers. He logged 132 miles in one week. He crossed the Continental Divide.

And he kept reminding himself: this journey was never just about the miles. It was about honoring his dad, his brother, and the countless people facing the slow, heartbreaking loss of Alzheimer's. It was about hope.
He closed the month with 2,311 miles behind him, and just under 700 to go.

"Still heading west," he wrote. "We all have our own west to head to. I've realized where mine is. And what I'm supposed to do on the way."

July 1, 2013

He was struggling…When I jogged through the heart of Albuquerque today a man caught my eye. He looked quiet and sad. I walked over near him, locked Wilson's brake and asked him how he was doing. He said "right now I am struggling"

He looked very tired, he looked very scared. I told him that I was just an old guy trying to help. No need to be afraid of me. I told him that usually people do struggle.

Governor Susana Martinez #ENDALZ She was in

Albuquerque, New Mexico talking about the Silver Alert Law that went into effect last night at Midnight. The law was used this morning for a gentleman with Alzheimer's disease that got lost. He was found within an hour.

Mayor Richard J. Berry of Albuquerque He was a pretty good athlete. He is a great guy.

July 2, 2013

Heading west and leaving Albuquerque, New Mexico.

Done for the day ... 19 miles..

This is hard, but.....I rest every night with no pressure. I can quit at any time and take this self-imposed task off of me.

Caregiving does not have that choice.

July 3, 2013

Albuquerque, New Mexico We will be heading West, one step at a time by 7:00 am.

Done for the day. July 3, 2013 2070 miles of the Journey are done. I have 950 miles left. Things are going well. Very mild temperatures today.

July 4, 2013

If I was home in North Georgia I would have woken up very early and headed to Woodstock, Ga. to see my grandson Tyler run in the annual 5k race. We would have then watched the parade and went to Waffle House to eat. Tonight, we would go to see fireworks.

My grandson Tyler !!

Hard Day Today I have done everything I could do to try and pretend I do not miss my family and friends. No matter what I do, I still miss them so much. This has been pretty tough since the first day, but I am still out here. I don't know how to not miss people and don't even know how I have been over 2000 miles, but I have. If I have ever made it look easy, that was by accident.

July 5, 2013

Still Heading West. !!

Not at 100% Woke up at about 87%. So, I got up and started heading West.

July 6th, 2013

Done for the day. Great day. Lot of folks stopping to talk.

Most talking about the disease, some about me doing this at

my age.

Thanks to all for the interest in an old guy (me) pushing a

baby stroller.

July 7, 2013

Not Running today. Gotta rest my body and mind.

Changed my mind…. Gonna go about 8 miles today.

July 8, 2013

Not feeling good!! I am not feeling very good. I do not feel as

strong as I have felt. The trip is getting harder, both mentally

and physically for me. I am renting a car tomorrow to take a

side trip for a couple of days. I will be driving to mile marker

16 on U.S. Highway 163 in Utah. This is where Forrest

Gump stopped running. Maybe there is something there, I am supposed to see or feel. I will then come back and finish the Journey.

July 9, 2013

Running for My Dad!!

Running where Forrest Gump ended his run.

Feeling pretty Strong here…..

July 10, 2013

Big Smiles for me Today!! Had a talk with my dad, and my

brother and was thinking of a promise I made to a doctor

about 8 years ago. I Did It Doc...... Thanks for the idea!!

July 11, 2013

The Journey is over... going home.... I have made the

decision to stop my journey Across the Land. I am going

home to Georgia. I do not have what it takes to finish. Each

day has been very hard lately. Some have said it is the heat,

some said the elevation change, some say I am pushing too

hard. Nonetheless, I have listened to my body and I have

made the decision to stop. Wilson and I have traveled 2,176 miles. Wilson carried the gear I needed, I pushed. We have been in Georgia, Alabama, Mississippi, Tennessee, Arkansas, Oklahoma, Texas and New Mexico. We have raised awareness for the Fight against Alzheimer's disease. We have raised money for the Alzheimer's Association. I did my best. So many people have helped me. Thank you very much.

I have met nothing but wonderful people all of the way. This is a beautiful country we live in. I will rest and then plan and then try with all of my heart to do what I planned. This decision was made by me alone. I love You!! Thanks for reading.

July 12, 2013

Wilson and I are heading east to Albuquerque, New Mexico this morning..

Not Going Home!! Going to rest and finish this Job!!

July 13, 2013

I am resting today, and the next few days in Albuquerque,

New Mexico. In a few days, I will get a ride back to Gallup,

New Mexico and then continue trying to get to Monterey,

California. I will try to have more discipline concerning my

planning and resting both my body and my mind. I enjoy

being alive. It is Awesome. It is….. Awesome.

July 14, 2013

Going to be a Great Day today. Resting my body and mind to

make the final assault on this trip.

July 15, 2013

I will continue to rest in Albuquerque, New Mexico.

July 16, 2013

Resting in Albuquerque, New Mexico

July 17, 2013

Just a few minutes Walking against traffic on I-40. There are trucks and cars going by a few feet away. Almost all of them move over to the inside lane if they can. Most of the people wave and tap their horns. I am listening to the iPod, watching for snakes and objects that could puncture Wilson's tires and watching traffic. A fast-paced song comes on my iPod and I begin to jog, not run, but jog. It is getting pretty hot, no wind today. I look around and there is no shade to be seen. I look up and in the distance I see some relief. I jog to it. It is an overpass. I get under it and stop, lock Wilson's brake and sit on the railing, drinking water or Gatorade.

In about 10 minutes, I unlock Wilson and start walking again. I wonder what my family and friends are doing. I am listening to the iPod.

July 18, 2013

Doing this in an attempt to fight Alzheimer's disease. When I sit across the table from him, I want to tell him I used everything he gave me.

Resting is helping me build my patience. Besides letting my body rest and my mind, I am building some patience I have not had much of. This is what I want to be doing right now. It is what I think is best for me.

July 19, 2013

Friday, July 19th 2013 Resting today in a Travelodge Motel on Route 66 in Gallup, New Mexico. The forecast is for a beautiful day.

Getting a lot of rest. Doing a lot of thinking. My body is starting to feel rested. The swelling has gone down a lot in my Achilles tendon. I feel good. I had lost some perspective; I think from being so tired. More rest is on tap for tomorrow and Sunday.

July 20, 2013

Guess what I am doing today? That is right, resting. Today and tomorrow and then Wilson and I go back to it again. In the Wilderness.

I am out in the middle of……..oh, never mind, you can see the motel…. shoot…

Fleet Feet – Easy Runner Little Rock, Arkansas Spoke to Sean this morning. He said the final 826 miles would be a walk in the park for me. The way he said it, sounded pretty good.

Resting is kind of hard. Sitting for so many days is kind of tough. I know I need it, but it takes a lot of discipline from me. One more day resting. Then Wilson and I head West. We have 826 miles to go.

July 21, 2013

Last day of resting before I start the final push to California. Looking forward to getting in Arizona.

We have been 2,176 miles and we have 826 miles left. Tomorrow, we will enter Arizona. I am very proud of what I have been through and still standing, still out here. The training miles plus the journey miles puts me at 4,816 miles in the last 12 months. 2,176 of it was pushing a jogging stroller. 4,816 miles divided by 52 weeks is 92 miles a week for the last year. That is the average.

July 22, 2013

Heading West to Arizona. :-)

If I stopped it would not be because I was hurting or exhausted, it would be because I could not take the pain or exhaustion anymore!!

I am just kiddin….. I could have swore I did 42.56 miles today…… but when the Dr. measured it in his truck it was just over 20. I am rounding up to 29. Just kiddin….. again. Marking it at 21. How can such flat land have hills? I did okay though. Still out here. Here comes Arizona, entered it today.

A new state…..Arizona

July 23, 2013

Still heading west. Wilson and I. What a team. Looking forward to a good day.

Done for the day. 27 miles. Road closings, bridge closings and 31 vehicles stopping to talk about this trip. Food and water given to me several times. I am in Chambers, Arizona.

July 24, 2013

The focus "Head West"

Yesterday's detour turned out to be very rewarding for me. It was an immediate uphill and the pavement disappeared. I started seeing homes and hearing dogs. The interstate noise slowly evaporated. People begin to stop. Most knew what I was doing, from reading the articles in the newspapers. A few folks came out from their homes to speak. I enjoyed them. Off and on there would be no homes and no traffic. There was just the peace that I feel sometimes in these type situations.

July 25, 2013

Heading west. Wilson and I. Still heading west…..

Running apparently makes your hair fall out

Still Heading West...... :-)

July 26, 2013

We will be heading towards Winslow, Arizona. We will

handle things as they come up.

July 27, 2013

Thanks for what you said to me.

I appreciate everything that was said to me when I very

seriously considered postponing the rest of the trip. I

appreciate everyone's passion and beliefs about what was best

for me. Nobody crossed the line, because with me, there is

not one. What you believe is what you believe and I can appreciate it very much. To every person that called, text or private messaged me, thank you for being concerned. I appreciate you!!

Done for the day..

WooooHooooo

2311 miles done…694 miles left….

We ran, jogged and walked 132 miles this week. Doing all of this to try and help in the fight against Alzheimer's disease. We are doing some good. Wooo Hooo

July 29, 2013

Over the next few days Wilson and I will be going from around 4800 feet above sea level to around 7000 feet above sea level. We will have to pay attention to the weather and I

186

will have to continue with the same management skills that got me over 137 miles last week and over 2,300 miles in the last 7 and 1/2 months. I will do the best I am capable of, which is what I have always done. What an Awesome life this is and has been.

Chapter 13
The Final Push
August 2013

August brought Jack closer to the Pacific Ocean, but not without some of the hardest, most soul-searching days of the entire journey. With over 2,400 miles behind him, he set his sights on California, but first, he had to cross some of the most unforgiving terrain of the entire trip. The Mojave Desert loomed ahead. So did questions about what finishing really meant.

Early in the month, Jack left Flagstaff, Arizona, knowing the miles ahead would be hotter, drier, and more desolate. Resources thinned out, and with temperatures soaring well into the triple digits, he had to make tough calls for safety. He accepted rides through parts of the Mojave making up the milage elsewhere, opting out of sections he deemed too dangerous to walk alone. It was a decision made not from weakness, but wisdom. He reminded himself, "This was never a track and field event. This is a fight against Alzheimer's."

Still, he continued pushing when he could. In places like Williams, Seligman, and Lake Havasu, he kept the conversation going, walking through towns multiple times a day, speaking with strangers about Alzheimer's, and handing out thousands of bracelets marked with the Alzheimer's Association's hotline: 1-800-272-3900.

On August 9th, Jack entered California, his tenth and final state. He had pushed himself over 2,500 miles on foot. He'd worn through nine pairs of shoes. His body was lighter, almost too lean, but his resolve remained strong.

Everywhere he went, he listened. A woman at a motel told him she used to hit her husband in frustration before realizing it was Alzheimer's. A Bible left on the bed with a five-dollar-bill tucked inside. A child from a French family who had followed his story online ran to give him a hug.

These weren't just miles; they were stories stitched into the road.

Even as he neared the coast, Jack's mind was already on what came next. He spoke of buying a car, wrapping it in Alzheimer's messaging, and retracing his route back east, visiting the very facilities, supporters, and Alzheimer's offices that had helped him along the way. He dreamed of one day standing in front of Congress and the National Alzheimer's Association to share what he had seen, what he had felt.

He called it "Team Across the Land 2013", and with their help, over $26,000 had already been raised, and Alzheimer's resources had been shared with millions.

On August 20th, Dad touched the Pacific Ocean for the first time in his life. It was an unofficial finish, a quiet, emotional moment with me on the phone and the sound of the waves crashing at his feet.

But the official end came on August 26th. Jack, with Wilson in front of him and a small crowd of supporters behind, made his final push to Bubba Gump Shrimp Company in Monterey, California. He had walked, jogged, and run 2,602 miles over the course of 226 days. He'd slept under tarps, in nursing homes, on borrowed beds, and in the homes of strangers-turned-friends. He had been changed.

He closed the chapter not with exhaustion, but with gratitude and conviction: "Still going and always will. Hey you, don't ever stop, no matter what occurs. I promise, I will not."

This journey was over, but Jack's mission, his hope, and his voice in the fight against Alzheimer's had only just begun.

August 1, 2013

Goodbye to a new friend. #ENDALZ She is 89 years old and recently lost her husband of over 60 years to a heart attack. He had Alzheimer's disease. She now has a dog named Willie. He is pretty cool. She saved him from being put to sleep. He saved her....... She loaned me her coffee pot and a cup, and a pot so I could boil water. She gave me some laundry detergent. It was hard telling her and Willie goodbye. She asked me if she could give me a hug. I said yes. She said "good luck on your journey" I said "good luck on yours"

August 2, 2013

California, here I come

August 3, 2013

The temperature at midnight in Needles was 101 degrees....

last night.....

The Miles 2,394 done 667 left Running, Jogging, walking and

talking..... 1-800-272-3900

When I announced I would Quit.... I put it on my blog and

Facebook and tweeted it. I went east 146 miles in a

car... When I changed my mind, I went 146 miles west in a

car. Then I started Running, Jogging, Walking again. Was I

embarrassed? No, not for a second, because it is never too

late!!

August 4, 2013

I figured out a way to never fail, never try.

Finished for the day....23 miles today. I dropped almost 1800 feet in elevation. I was on Interstate 40 most of the day. The highest temperature I was in was around 82 degrees. I had a little rain fall on me today. Talked with 2 bicycle riders crossing our Awesome country. Heading east…..

August 5, 2013

#ENDALZ I am wearing the shirt. Wilson is holding up the signs. We are telling folks about the disease known as Alzheimer's disease. 1-800-272-3900. Anytime…..

Done for the day… 24 miles, rough for me

August 6, 2013

No running today. Going to stay in Seligman and go around talking to folks about Alzheimer's.

Each of us has a fire in our hearts burning for something. It's our responsibility in life to find it and keep it lit. This is your life, and it's a short one. Don't let others extinguish your flame. Try what you want to try. Go where you want to go. Follow your own intuition. Dream with your eyes open until you know exactly what it looks like. Then do at least one thing every day to make it a reality.

August 7, 2013

Being in nursing homes and Alzheimer's units was rough on me. Emotionally it beat me up. Seeing the pain, the hurt and depression. This was a once in a while thing for me. Who could stand to be near this? Caregivers do, some 24 hours a day, 7 days a week and some for years. They do it out of love,

but I bet it is still hard.....I think they need a break. 1-800-272-3900. Anytime. Find a cure by 2020.

August 8, 2013

Why in the Mojave area, in August? #ENDALZ This arrival time was not planned. I never set down with pen and paper at a desk and made a conscious decision to get here in this heat. I arrived here now because of a couple of different circumstances. I will not be able to say I did every foot, because I will ride, in a car, through some of this heat, that I have decided, to drive through. I will not make the list of cross-country runners, joggers and walkers. Although, that would have been cool. I will not be on the list on the awesome USA Crossers page. Was it worth it to me? ABSOLUTELY, it is what the whole trip is for. This is a trip to Fight Alzheimer's disease. 1-800-272-3900. Anytime

Tomorrow, Wilson and I will enter California. We will enter the last state in a car. We will not be Running the 189 miles from Kingman, Arizona to Barstow, California. Once we reach Barstow, we will get out of the car, get into a motel, for a couple of days and plan the last part of the trip. Today, in Lake Havasu, Arizona. I can see California from here.

I have been 2,495 miles on foot, on this trip. I have pushed Wilson almost all of them.

August 9, 2013

My grandson Tyler told me before I left "Papa, if something happens and you can't walk anymore, I will push you in a shopping cart to California".

A new state…..California 2013

Across the Land 2013. #ENDALZ 2,508 miles. That is the miles I have been on foot, Running, Jogging and Walking. I have been by myself, no support vehicle. Raising money for the Alzheimer's Association and letting the public know the Alzheimer's Association exists. This has been very hard. I have persisted. I am in California. This is the tenth state I have been in. I started in Savannah, Georgia. I am heading to Monterey, California.

August 11, 2013

So Longs are difficult!!

Today is an Anniversary When today is over, I will have been on this trip for 7 months. I am very tired emotionally and physically. It has been worth it. I hoped it has helped someone or something......

We met with 4 Governors. We met with one Assistant Governor. We met 3 Mayors. We were recognized in the Oklahoma State Senate. In Albuquerque, New Mexico, we were honored with a proclamation giving us a Jack Fussell, Alzheimer's Association Day. At each of these events the name Alzheimer's Association was mentioned and sometimes several times.

My Friend .....

August 12, 2013

Heading North. #ENDALZ that's right, North. Heading to

Monterey, California….. 7 months ago, I left Savannah, Georgia Still Going…..

August 14, 2013

Never Quit, Never Give Up. Finish !!

I finally understand. #ENDALZ If you call a newspaper or tv crew and ask them to meet you on the side of the road or at a beach and they know you work for the Alzheimer's Association or any other organization, they probably will say no, not this time. So, no air or print time to notify the public the Association exists. But if you call and say you have a 62-year-old man, pushing a jogging stroller by himself across most of the country, they usually will come out and the Alzheimer's Association gets air or print time. That lets the public know the Alzheimer's Association exists and that they will help them. It lets the public know they can contribute. It lets the government know the problem is getting bigger. So, it really does help. It is your turn. I are tired…..:-)

August 15, 2013

Thanks Wilson. You have been Amazing

Time to eat. I am 6 foot tall. I have gotten a little too slim. I

weighed 144 lbs. this morning. I weighed 155 lbs., when I

started the trip.

August 16, 2013

Just wanted to. I ran 2 miles in Colorado. I ran 3 miles in

Utah. I ran 1 mile into the Mojave National Preserve. I Ran,

Jogged and Walked over 2,500 miles, with no support,

pushing a jogging stroller. I weighed between 240-272 for 25

years. I will be 63 years old on October the 8th. It is never

too late to change…..

August 17, 2013

A Dream. What happens when you complete a dream? Well,

you just start thinking about another one.....

August 18, 2013

Almost there...... #ENDALZ

$26,000.00. #ENDALZ for the Alzheimer's Association to help people...... that need help so much.....

37 miles to Monterey, California. #ENDALZ

Can I push a jogging stroller 2,600 miles in 226 days? Can I do this without having a support team on the ground with me? Can I quit two times, but never stop and keep on going?

Could you do things that seem too hard to do? YES, to all of these questions!!

A bunch of 1/2 marathons Even with all of the days I did not run, we will have averaged running, jogging and walking almost a 1/2 marathon every day for 226 days, while pushing a jogging stroller with gear in it. I took very few days off. Most of the day's I did not run, jog and walk, I was attending facilities or events with the Alzheimer's Association. Some of the days, I was visiting with nursing homes or assisted living facilities. I spent 5 days driving home to see my mom and her husband, who was very sick, in the hospital, after I rented a car. I assure anyone reading this, if I can do that, you can too.....

August 19, 2013

How much was donated daily? $118.00 every day. That is $26,000.00, to help the Alzheimer's Association, help people......

Done for the day…19 miles today. Sunny and mild today. Ran through a lot of places that grow vegetables. 1-800-272-3900. Anytime

August 20, 2013

Milestone – unofficial finish of the Epic Journey 2013

This trip was supposed to end in Monterey, but there's a problem with that, the ocean, that's the culprit, it's a Bay in Monterey, not the ocean. Although this has not been an "every foot on foot" trip, I still want to go ocean to ocean. Been thinking about that the last few days. Well today, it worked itself out.

I called my daughter to tell her I would be near the ocean, in Marina, at my home for the night, the Motel 6. We realized together that I would be less than 1/2 mile from the ocean, when I am in room for the night.

So, I didn't wait, I talked on the phone, with my daughter as I topped the hill, and for the first time in my life, there was the Pacific Ocean in front of me. I walked on down and touched the water just as I did at the Atlantic Ocean. A kind lady took this photo.

This was the "real" finish, but the official one will be at Bubba Gump's in Monterey.

August 21, 2013

3000 bracelets. #ENDALZ I gave out over 3000 purple bracelets on this trip. The bracelets had a phone number on them. 1-800-272-3900. Anytime

7 months and 9 days Wilson and I have been speaking the word Alzheimer's. The word is on my shirt, my cap, Wilson's sign and on the over 3000 bracelets we gave away. The 1-800-272-3900 number was on the bracelets. I said the word every time I ate at a restaurant and at every motel or campground. We have to find a cure. 1-800-272-3900. Anytime

August 22, 2013

Morning. Will do a quick, short jog around the neighborhood. Wilson will sleep in. Just me and the iPod. Breakfast at 8:00 am with some very Awesome people. Going to Relax some.....

I'm pretty tired. I think I'll go home now.....

I made it.

August 23, 2013

Hope, is a Miracle!! #ENDALZ The sadness on the faces can rip your heart out. If you have the ability to make someone smile, a real smile, in my opinion, you have performed a miracle.

August 24, 2013

In Monterey, California. Wilson and I are relaxing.

August 25, 2013

2.6 miles left on the Journey. #ENDALZ August 26, I will leave the Mariposa Motel and take Wilson 2.6 miles to Bubba Gump Shrimp Factory for a Celebration.

August 26, 2013

My running buddies have arrived

The G.M. of Bubba Gump

Chapter 14

More than Miles

The numbers are staggering. In 2013, Jack Fussell ran, jogged, and walked/ran over 2,600 miles across ten states with a single goal: to raise awareness and support for those impacted by Alzheimer's disease.

But the real story lies in what those miles *meant*. During his 226-day journey, Jack handed out over 3,000 purple bracelets, each imprinted with the Alzheimer's Association's 24/7 helpline, 1-800-272-3900. He said that number out loud in interviews, on sidewalks, in nursing homes, at rest stops, and in small-town diners. It showed up over 80 times in his blog.

He said the word Alzheimer's 753 times and used #ENDALZ 400 times, not because it boosted his visibility, but because it kept the mission in the spotlight, where it belonged.

During this run, he raised $27,000 in direct donations to the Alzheimer's Association. He completed 22 TV interviews, 55 newspaper interviews, 12 radio appearances, and was featured in 5 magazines all to bring awareness to Alzheimer's disease.

He did this without a team, without a big name, without a sponsor. Just Jack. Just Wilson. Just a mission. And he wasn't done.

After reaching Monterey, Jack didn't rest for long. In 2015, he set out again, this time running another cross-country journey. When he wasn't walking, he was *driving the route*, revisiting care facilities, Alzheimer's offices, and the people who had supported his cause. His car became a moving billboard for awareness, proudly bearing the Alzheimer's hotline and messages of hope.

Wherever he went, he wore his cap and shirt with pride. He always made time to talk. He *cared* deeply, endlessly, and without pause. His life was never aimless. He always had a mission.

To those who followed his journey, donated, gave him rides, cheered him on from sidewalks, and shared your stories, thank you. Your love carried him. Your encouragement fueled him. Your stories stayed with him.

And in honor of Jack's unwavering belief in the power of information, if you or someone you love is living with Alzheimer's, or if you simply need support, help is available right now.

Call the Alzheimer's Association Helpline at 1-800-272-3900. It's free. It's confidential. It's always open.

Jack believed one voice could make a difference. And he was right. He proved that every mile matters. Every conversation counts. And every act of love leaves a footprint.

This was Across the Land. And in the echoes of every footstep, Jack lives on. He will never be forgotten.